O9-BHJ-901

Virginia

VIRGINIA BY ROAD

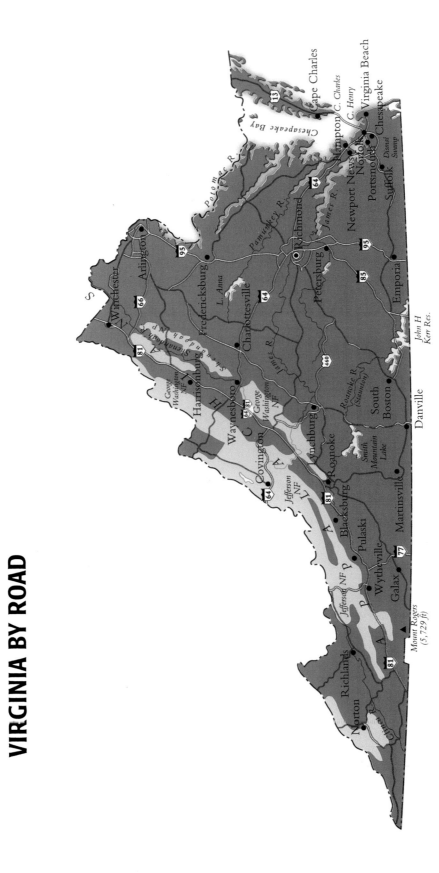

Celebrate the States

Virginia

Tracy Barrett

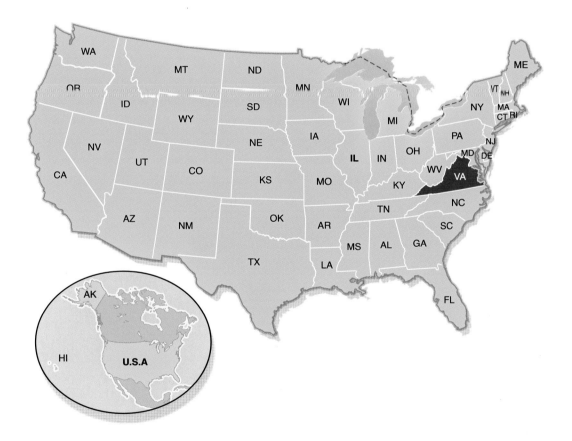

Marshall Cavendish
Benchmark
New York

For Greg, Laura, Beth, and Patrick

Marshall Cavendish Benchmark
99 White Plains Road
Tarrytown, New York 10591-9001
www.marshallcavendish.us

Library of Congress Cataloging-in-Publication Data

Barrett, Tracy, 1955–
Virginia / Tracy Barrett.— 2nd ed.
p. cm. — (Celebrate the states)
Summary: Discusses the geographic features, history, government, people,
and attractions of the state known as the Mother of Presidents.
Includes bibliographical references and index.
ISBN 0-7614-1734-6
1. Virginia—Juvenile literature. [1. Virginia.] I. Title. II. Series.
F226.3.B35 2004   975.5—dc22   2003014926

Series design by Adam Mietlowski

Photo research by Candlepants Incorporated

Cover photo: Getty Images/Stone

The photographs in this book are used by permission and through the courtesy of: *The Image
Works:* Jim West, 8; Sonda Dawes, 11, 21, 58, 80, 118; Townsend P. Dickenson, 12; Jenny Hager,
19; Jeff Greenberg, 50, 98, 108; Steven Rubin, 53, 61, 89; David Wells, 55; Joe Sohm, 68; Michael
Geissinger, 97. *Photo Researchers, Inc.:* Brian Yarvin, 15; Richard T. Nowitz, 76, 103. *Corbis:* 39, 47,
129. Lynda Richardson, 19, 22; Stapleton Collection, 27; Bettmann, 30, 32, 33, 36, 73, 122, 127,
128; Richard T. Nowitz, 35, 119; Katherine Karnow, 42; Tim Wright, 49; David Stoeklein, 56; John
Henley, 64; Dave Bartruff, 66; Tim Wright, 78; Kevin Fleming, 82; Ted Horowitz, 87; David Sallors,
90; Gary W. Carter, 111; Buddy Mays, 114; Austrian Archives, 123; Bureau L.A. Collection, 124;
The Corcoran Gallery of Art, 125. *Art Resource:* Giraudon, 24; SCALA, 41. *Getty Images:* Photodisc
Green, 85; National Geographic, 92, 94-95; Photographers Choice, 100; Stone, 105, 131, 136;
Reportage, 107, back cover; The Image Bank, 113; Photodisc Graan, 120.

Printed in China
3 5 6 4 2

Contents

Virginia Is . . .

Virginia is beautiful land . . .

"Equal to the promised land in fertility, and far superior to it for beauty."
—author Washington Irving

"Heaven and earth never agreed better to frame a place for man's habitation. Here are hills, plains, valleys, rivers and brooks, all running most pleasantly into a faire bay encompassed about with fruitful and delightsome land."
—Captain John Smith

"Looking out my back door, I see so many shades of green that I can't even begin to count them. And then the birds start to sing, and I stand there and think, this is Heaven."
—Virginia native Penny Waldron

. . . and proud people.

"I like your country, Virginia, and Virginians. Virginians are all snobs. I like snobs. A snob spends so much time being a snob he has none left to bother other people."
—author William Faulkner

"In Virginia, all the geese think they are swans."
—President John Adams

"Am I proud to be a Virginian? I would be ashamed to be anything else!"
—Sara Bell

Virginians love politics . . .

"I am a Virginian, so naturally I am a politician."
—Nancy Astor, speech in England, 1919

. . . and above all, they love their state.

"You can work for Virginia, to build her up again, to make her great again. You can teach your children to love and cherish her."
—Confederate general Robert E. Lee to a young girl,
five years after the end of the Civil War

"Good Old Dominion, the blessed mother of us all."
—President Thomas Jefferson

"No one should ever ask a man whether he was born in Virginia because, if he was, he certainly will tell you himself, and if he was not, he will be ashamed to admit it."
—William Cabell Bruce

Virginia is history: The American Revolution started and ended there, and the Civil War was fought most bitterly within its borders. Virginia was the first of the thirteen colonies. The original Virginia colony was carved up into many future states (Kentucky, Ohio, Indiana, Illinois, Michigan, Wisconsin, Minnesota, and West Virginia), giving it the nickname the Mother of States. Eight presidents were born there, making it the Mother of Presidents as well.

Virginia is also government: Many of the people who work for the federal government in Washington, D.C., live there. Virginia is beautiful beaches, rolling farmland, and mountains; small towns, busy cities, and quiet country-side. It is people with many kinds of jobs and varied interests. Virginia is home to people of different backgrounds living together, working hard to make their state the best it can be.

Chapter One

"A Glorious Paradise"

Rolling hills, green meadows, glittering beaches, salt marshes—Virginia's varied geography has always been one of its main attractions for visitors and residents alike. Thomas Jefferson, a native of the state, said in 1791, "When we consider how much climate contributes to the happiness of our condition, . . . we have reason to value highly the accident of birth in such a one as that of Virginia." Most modern Virginians would agree with him. The delightful variety is due to a combination of geological accidents that began 300 million years ago.

In that ancient time, two flat pieces of the earth's surface, called tectonic plates, started to rub against each other under the vast sea that covered much of what is now Virginia. Although they moved incredibly slowly—just inches a year—they pressed against each other so hard and for so long that over the course of 50 million years they rose up from the ocean. The sea receded, and eventually their great ridges formed the Appalachian Mountains. These mountains run along much of the eastern United States, including the western part

Hikers pause along the Appalachian Trail to admire the view of the Shenandoah Valley from their perch high above.

of Virginia. The sharp peaks wore down over millions of years so that today they are gently rolling hills, blanketed with plants and trees and full of animals.

The lush fertility of Virginia is not a recent development. Millions of years ago, it must have been one of the liveliest spots on Earth. Many dinosaur fossils have been found there. The coal deposits in the western part of the state are the fossilized remains of huge ancient forests. The limestone that runs under much of the state is made up of the fossilized bodies of the sea creatures that once lived in the prehistoric sea.

Later, when the first mammals roamed the earth, Virginia became a busy crossroads of early life. Large numbers of mastodon fossils have been found there. In his *Notes on the State of Virginia,* Thomas Jefferson said that Native American mythology identified these bones as the remains of monsters killed by Indian heroes. Excavations in the Saltville Valley show that mastodons were probably butchered, cooked, and eaten there about 14,000 years ago—at least 2,500 years before many anthropologists had first thought humans lived in the Americas. Not only did people most likely live there, but they also made tools very early in prehistory. Jerry N. McDonald, who led the Saltville excavation, found what he considers to be a human-made tool, saying that "it could have served as a combined cutting edge and a wedge to slip in between layers of meat or to separate meat from bone."

In prehistoric times the coast of Virginia reached far out into the Atlantic Ocean. But when the polar icecaps melted at the end of the last Ice Age, the level of the ocean rose and flooded the land, slowly pushing the shoreline inland—close to where it now lies. To this day, the eastern coast of the state is so low in altitude that much of it is marshland and thus floods frequently.

Virginia is fairly small. At 42,769 square miles, it ranks thirty-fifth among the fifty states. Its shape reminds some people of an old-fashioned lady's slipper, with its toe pointing to the west and its heel on the bay. At the top of the slipper sits Washington, D.C. The state is bounded on the east by the Atlantic Ocean and the Chesapeake Bay, and it shares its other borders with five states: Maryland (and Washington, D.C.) to the northeast, West Virginia to the west and northwest, Kentucky to the west, and Tennessee and North Carolina to the south.

MANY VIRGINIAS

Virginia can be divided into three main regions: the Tidewater on the east (including the Eastern Shore), the central Piedmont, and the western Mountain and Valley region.

One of the best ways to see nature in Virginia is to take a canoe ride in Chesapeake Bay.

IN CELEBRATION OF BIRDS AND OYSTERS

The natural beauties of the Eastern Shore make it a good place to celebrate wildlife. Bird lovers flock to the three-day Eastern Shore Birding Festival each October to watch the migration of hundreds of songbirds, as well as the larger hawks and falcons. In November parts of the wildlife refuge on Assateague Island that are usually off-limits to humans are open to the public for its annual Waterfowl Week. There bird-watchers get the chance to observe waterfowl migration at its peak.

The oysters that provide a livelihood for so many residents of the Eastern Shore are also celebrated in October. Chincoteague Island plays host to its Oyster Festival, where bands perform as people eat oysters and other local seafood.

The Tidewater

Many rivers and creeks flow into the ocean in the eastern part of the state. They divide the land into long, narrow peninsulas, called necks by the locals. The tidal flows of the ocean enter the wide mouths of many of the rivers, giving the region the nickname the Tidewater. The ocean water makes the rivers brackish, or salty, and has created many swamps. The largest is the 63,000-acre Great Dismal Swamp. To the early settlers, accustomed to England's green fields and thick forests, this marsh with its snakes, mosquitoes, and unfamiliar creatures must certainly have seemed gloomy, or dismal. But to American-born George Washington, the Great Dismal Swamp was "a glorious paradise." His opinion is shared by many Virginians today.

The southern tip of the Eastern Shore is a flat, sandy, windswept area. This narrow strip of land hangs almost due south, cutting off Chesapeake Bay from the ocean. It is called the Delmarva peninsula, a name created by combining parts of "DELaware," "MARyland," and "VirginiA," the three states that share it. Many islands cluster around this large peninsula.

The Piedmont

The Piedmont (from two Italian words meaning "mountain foot") covers the central part of the state. In this region, the land rises gently from the eastern lowlands to the mountains farther to the west. The rolling foothills are fertile and covered with forests. Most of the trees are the same species that grew in the area centuries ago. There are a few pines and many hardwoods, such as oak and maple.

The Piedmont is watered by numerous rivers, including the Potomac, the Rappahannock, the York, and the James. These rivers flow southeast on their way out of the hills.

Mountain and Valley Region

The Appalachian Mountains rise out of the Piedmont foothills. This vast chain is divided into different sections, including the Alleghenies and the Blue Ridge Mountains, so called because the moist air rising out of them makes their ridges look blue-green. Lara Semones, who grew up in the Blue Ridge Mountains, says, "From any mountaintop, no matter what time of day, they have a blue hue to them." The western mountains also hold the lovely Shenandoah Valley. The Shenandoah, Clinch, and New rivers add their moisture to this lush region as well.

A PLEASANT CLIMATE AND BEAUTIFUL BIRDS

Virginia has generally warm weather, although it tends to be cooler in the mountains than in the low-lying areas. Along the shore, temperatures of 50° Fahrenheit in midwinter are not uncommon, and the thermometer can go to well above 90° F for much of the summer. Many people, both Virginians and visitors, take advantage of the hot and usually sunny summer weather to spend a lot of time at the beach. Norfolk's average temperature runs from 47° F in January to a high of 86° F in July.

The area around Washington, D.C., tends to be hotter and wetter. Gordon Duffus of Chester points out, "Our nation's capital was built in a swamp." The heat and humidity can combine to make summers in northern Virginia steamy and uncomfortable.

In the mountains the weather is drier than in the Piedmont and especially in the Tidewater, where the warm ocean breezes bring high humidity ashore. The mountains also display their spectacular fall foliage, attracting residents and tourists alike to view the trees as they turn dazzling colors. Lara Semones says, "The climate is wonderful. We have four distinct seasons—the fall is yellow and red and orange.

A new day begins on a farm near Galax, along the Blue Ridge Parkway.

Lots of people like to ride their bikes along the Blue Ridge Parkway and just look at the colors. The winter, with the snow, is really gorgeous. You can see forever. There's dogwood everywhere in the spring. Summertime is hot and humid from July on. Everything is so green, and the farmland is just beautiful."

Rainfall is moderate throughout the state, as is snowfall. Even in the mountains it is rare for more than 2 or 3 feet to fall in one winter.

People in Virginia take advantage of this pleasant climate: They swim in the ocean and the bay, hike, explore caves, and boat in the Piedmont and Mountain and Valley region. Given Virginia's varied geography and mild climate, it is not surprising that many different kinds of animals and plants thrive in the state. More than half of the state is covered with dense forest, where deer and bear, as well as smaller mammals, find food and shelter.

White-tailed deer have adapted well to life in Virginia, with its open spaces and plentiful food.

LAND AND WATER

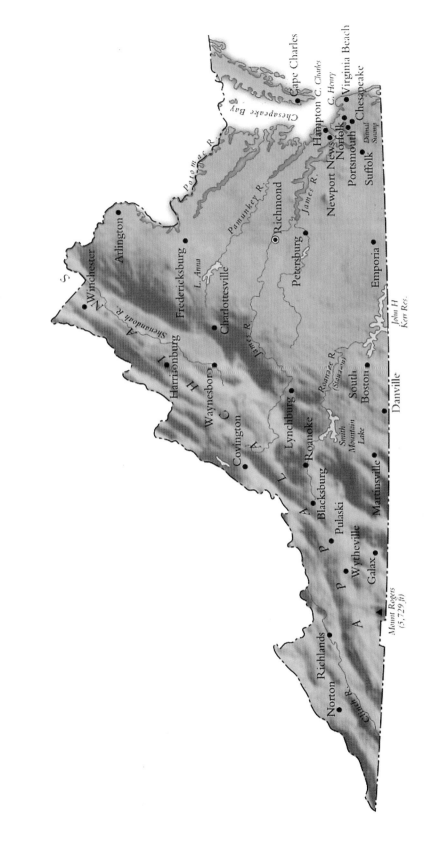

The trees provide a home for many varieties of birds, ranging in size from large wild turkeys to brilliant red cardinals, the state bird. Many of these birds have feathers of spectacular colors, especially the orioles, scarlet tanagers, blue grosbeaks, and ruby-throated hummingbirds. Since most birds are shy, catching a glimpse of their brilliant plumage through the trees is a rare treat.

The Eastern Shore is also home to many birds—snow geese, herons, bald eagles, pelicans, falcons, and ducks—that depend on the sea for their

THREATENED LIVES

Slender chub, duskytail darter, Cumberland monkeyface mussel, tan riffleshell, shiny pigtoe, sensitive joint-vetch, Virginia sneeze-weed, small whorled pogonia—they all sound like the names invented for animals and plants that don't actually exist. And someday they may be just that: names that don't belong to any real living thing, because they are among Virginia's threatened and endangered species.

Sometimes plants and animals run the risk of extinction because of their beauty. The swamp pink is threatened not only because development is reducing its habitat, but because gardeners dig up plants growing in the wild to transplant to their own gardens. The swamp pink reproduces slowly, so when any single plant dies, it takes a long time to be replaced.

Protected areas have been set aside for the swamp pink, and people found harming one of these plants may be fined, even if the flower is on their own private property.

A transmitter has been glued to the back of this Atlantic loggerhead turtle. It does not harm the animal and allows scientists to track and study its movements.

food and are larger than the forest birds. They are drawn to the ocean, where a lucky visitor can spot giant sea turtles, dolphins, and whales. Huge fish called shad are also found in the rivers and ocean.

Unfortunately for these and other animals and plants, the attractions of Virginia have brought in many people, leading to the destruction of much of the habitat. Local industries have also polluted much of the remaining land and water. Non-native species move in and compete with other plants and animals for resources. In 2003 fifty animals and thirteen plants in Virginia were listed as either threatened or endangered.

"THE GREATEST PEOPLE IN THE WORLD"

Unitarian minister William Ellery Charming said in the 1830s that if the Virginians could only do without their slaves, he would "think them the greatest people in the world." Many people still think of Virginians as great and want to share in what the state has to offer. The state's population rose 14.4 percent between 1990 and 2000, with most growth in the northern part of the state and the least in the southwestern area. The U.S. government estimates that in 2001, 7,187,734 people lived in Virginia, making it the twelfth most populated state in the country.

Historically this figure marks a population decline. Virginia was originally the most populous of the thirteen colonies, and then was the most populous state for decades. By 1820 it had dropped to third place, then to seventh by 1860. Much of the drop is due to the fact that Virginia did not have many factories until the twentieth century, long after major industrialization occurred in the northeastern part of the United States. The immigrants who came to America in the nineteenth century were looking for industrial work. Since Virginia had few factories, most of them settled in the North instead.

Where people live in the state has changed as well. In 1900 few Virginians were city dwellers. Most were farmers or fishermen, who lived in small towns or in the country. But by 1955 more than half of the population had settled in the cities. Now nearly three-quarters of Virginians live in large cities, 10 percent in small cities, and only 20 percent in the country.

The growth in the state's population has not always been good for the environment. Chesapeake Bay has long provided a livelihood for people who support themselves by fishing, but recently the bay has become over-fished. Sea life has deteriorated greatly in this century, due mostly to the pollution funneling into the bay.

A sixty-one-year-old waterman harvests his catch of blue crabs caught in the Chesapeake Bay.

This student at the Virginia Institute of Marine Science takes samples of blue crabs from the York River. Studying the state's rivers is the best way to learn how to protect and preserve Virginia's valuable resources.

Forty-eight rivers empty into the bay. These rivers flow through heavily populated areas on their way to the shore and carry with them industrial waste and the runoff of fertilizer from farms. The fertilizer encourages algae to grow so quickly and so abundantly that it reduces the amount of oxygen available to the fish, causing them to die. Their rotting bodies make the water even more unclean. Few people even swim in the bay anymore.

Cleanup efforts have begun but still have a long way to go. Virginians are aware that all creatures living in or near the rivers depend on a delicate balance. For their continuing survival, and that of the people who share their world, the waterways must be kept clean.

Chapter Two

The Colonie of Virginia

The first humans arrived in what is now Virginia thousands of years ago—exactly when is the source of some discussion. In 2000 excavations at Cactus Hill, in southeastern Virginia, stirred up a heated debate among archaeologists. Most scholars had thought that people had arrived there between five and eight thousand years ago. But discoveries at Cactus Hill, including several spear points, indicate that people may have been living there as far back as fifteen thousand years ago.

The land these people knew looked quite different from how it appears today. During the last Ice Age, so much of the earth's water was locked in icy glaciers that the sea level was lower. Thick pine and fir forests covered the land, only to retreat to the north as the climate warmed and the hardwoods of today began to take over. The coasts were flooded as the glaciers melted. Huge animals such as mastodons and mammoths were wiped out by a combination of changes in the environment and overhunting.

Virginia's first residents were the Native Americans who settled the region, eventually fanning out across the future state.

Most humans in the Americas at that time moved from place to place, hunting, fishing, and gathering plants along the way. At some time long ago, they began to return to the same place year after year rather than migrate from one spot to another. They burned trees and brush in a small area and allowed the ashes to gather on the ground. This ashy buildup helped change the chemical makeup of the soil, so the next year berry bushes and other plants would grow better. When the people returned the next summer, they found they had more berries and seeds to pick and eat. They started leaving ashes behind on purpose, and some groups eventually moved on to planting seeds and cultivating crops.

It was about four thousand years ago that Virginia's first permanent residents settled down long enough to grow crops. They cleared land in the river valleys and near the sea, built houses, and hunted game. Two major changes at around that time increased the first Virginians' food supply and well-being: the invention of pottery and the widespread use of the bow and arrow. With pots, food could be stored and cooked more efficiently; and the bow and arrow made it easier to hunt game from a distance.

Several different tribes lived, for the most part, peacefully in different parts of the state. In the east were the Susquehanna and the largest group, the Powhatan. In the center were the Monacan and Manahoac, while to the west the Cherokee reigned. Sometimes these groups cooperated with one another, but many times they guarded their own resources and refused to allow others access to them.

Most of the tribes in what is now Virginia spoke the Algonquian language. Members of this group numbered about 14,000 to 21,000 at the time of European contact. The other two main groups were speakers of Iroquoian and Siouan languages. Many of their villages were located near rivers where the fishing was good. They usually lived in houses made of

Europeans were intrigued by the boat-making techniques of some Native Americans. This image was published in 1590, feeding the European curiosity about the people in the "New World."

saplings lashed together and covered with bark. The speakers of Algonquian called the Eastern Shore *Accawmacke,* so the early English mapmakers referred to Virginia as "the Colonie of Virginia and the Kingdom of Accawmacke."

THE JAMESTOWN SETTLEMENT

Giovanni da Verrazano, an Italian who explored for the French government, was the first European to pass through Virginia, in about 1524. Fifty years later Spanish priests founded a settlement on the York River, but they did not stay long.

GLOOSCAP AND THE BABY—AN ALGONQUIAN TALE

Glooscap [both the first man and a god], having conquered the Kewawkqu', a race of giants and magicians, the Medecolin, who were cunning sorcerers, and Pamola, a wicked spirit of the night, besides a host of fiends, goblins, cannibals, and witches, felt himself great indeed, and boasted to a woman that there was nothing left for him to subdue.

But the woman laughed and said: "Are you quite sure, Master? There is still one who remains unconquered, and nothing can overcome him."

Surprised at this, Glooscap inquired the name of such a mighty one.

"He is called Wasis," replied the woman, "but I strongly advise you to have no dealings with him."

Wasis was only a baby, who sat on the floor sucking a piece of maple sugar and humming a little song to himself. Glooscap had never married, so he was ignorant of how children are best managed. But with perfect confidence he smiled at the baby and asked him to come to him. The baby smiled but never moved, whereupon Glooscap imitated a beautiful birdsong. Wasis, however, paid no attention and went on sucking his maple sugar. Unaccustomed to such treatment, Glooscap flew into a rage and in a terrible and threatening tone ordered Wasis to come to him at once. But Wasis burst into loud howls, which drowned the god's thundering, and would not budge despite the threats.

Glooscap, thoroughly angered, summoned all his magical resources. He recited the most terrible spells and the most dreadful incantations. He sang the songs that raised the dead and those that send the devil scurrying to the nethermost depths. But Wasis merely smiled and looked a little bit bored.

At last Glooscap rushed from the hut in despair, while Wasis, sitting on the floor, gurgled, "Goo, goo!" And to this day the Indians say that when babies say "Goo," they are remembering when they conquered mighty Glooscap.

The explorers liked what they saw, though. The woods were so thick that, as one historian has said, "in the seventeenth century, a squirrel could have crossed eastern North America from the Mississippi River to the Atlantic Ocean without touching the ground." There was abundant game, and the explorers had never before seen such enormous seafood— lobsters six feet long, for example. As Thomas Jefferson was to say more than a century later, "This scene is worth a voyage across the Atlantic."

An early English traveler was of the same opinion, writing to the king enthusiastically: "If Virginia had but horses and kine [cattle] in some reasonable proportion, I dare assure myself, being inhabited with English, no realm in Christendom were comparable to it."

In 1585 the English claimed the area and named it Virginia in honor of Queen Elizabeth I, the Virgin Queen. In 1606 King James I gave the land to the Virginia Company. The settlers were ordered to explore, build a settlement, and convert the natives to Christianity. They landed at what is now Virginia Beach on April 26, 1607.

The settlers' first meeting with the native peoples seems to have frightened everyone. The settlers saw half-naked men "creeping upon all fours . . . like bears, with their bows in their mouths, [who] charged us very desperately in the faces." When the settlers fired their rifles, the Indians, who had never heard gunshots before, ran in terror.

The English settlers' first impressions of the land, on the other hand, were very positive. One traveler wrote of "faire meddowes and goodly tall trees, with such Fresh Waters running through the woods as I was almost ravished at the first sight thereof." The newcomers, pleased with their prospects, built Jamestown, England's first permanent American town.

Researchers have long thought that the original Jamestown fort had been washed into the James River. But archaeologists who began excavating

In this romanticized portrayal of the landing at Jamestown, Virginia, there is no hint of the conflict that would eventually arise between the settlers and the Native Americans.

in 1994 soon discovered its remains on the banks of the river, along with artifacts and several burial sites. Among their discoveries is the skeleton of a young white man whose leg bone had been shattered by a bullet. He most likely died of loss of blood or an infection from the wound. Another skeleton, originally unearthed in the 1940s, was reexamined and found to belong to an African man in his midtwenties. He too was the victim of a bullet wound, but this time to the head. Were these accidents? Murders? Further excavations may provide clues.

Despite its beauty, Jamestown turned out to be a bad choice for a place to build a town. The water was bad, and the land was swampy and filled with mosquitoes that carried disease. The colonists had come mostly from cities and did not know how to farm, build houses, or hunt.

To add to their hardships, they happened to arrive in what they called the New World just as a major drought was devastating the growing seasons. Recent investigation of tree rings has shown that for seven years, the rainfall in the area was drastically low. According to Dennis Blanton, director of the William and Mary Center for Archaeological Research, "If the English had tried to find a worse time to launch their settlements in the New World, they could not have done so."

If it had not been for the help offered by the local Powhatan Indians, it is almost certain that none of the colonists would have survived.

The settlers depended especially on two strong people. One was their leader, Captain John Smith, a short, strong redhead only twenty-seven years old. He made maps of the region, adopting many of the Indian names, such as Chesapeack, meaning "great shellfish bay." The other person was Pocahontas, the daughter of the Indian leader Powhatan. Smith described Powhatan as "a tall well proportioned man, with a sower [sour] look." Once Powhatan captured Smith. Smith probably made up the now-famous story that Pocahontas saved his life, but she did convince her father to be kind to the settlers on several occasions. Despite her willingness to help the settlers, the English kidnapped her in 1613.

Smith was injured in a gunpowder explosion and had to return to England. Without his steady leadership, the colony faced serious trouble. By the end of their first year, more than two-thirds of the colonists had died. More settlers arrived in 1609, but the situation became even grimmer. They had so little food in the winter of 1609–1610 that about 435 of the 500 residents died before spring. One survivor said: "Our men were destroyed with cruell diseases as Swellings, Fluxes, Burning Fevers . . . but for the most part

George Percy, who followed John Smith as the leader of the Virginia colony, called his predecessor "an Ambityous unworthy and vayne-glorious [proud] fellowe."

they died of meere famine." That winter became known as the "starving time."

Even so, more colonists came in 1610. The Indians had taught them how to plant crops, but by then the English had realized how much money could be made growing tobacco. Until this time, the plant had been unknown outside the Americas, but as soon as Europeans discovered snuff, chewing tobacco, and pipes, they immediately wanted more. So instead of planting food, the settlers concentrated on tobacco. People became so eager to make profits off the popular crop that they even planted seeds in the cracks of the streets!

Even in those days, not everyone approved of tobacco. King James called smoking a "custom loathsome to the eye, hateful to the nose, harmful to the brain, dangerous to the lungs." But royal disapproval was not enough to make people ignore the enormous profits to be made from this plant that contains addictive substances. A colonist named John Rolfe found a way to cure, or dry, leaves for export to Europe. He became extremely wealthy. He married Pocahontas in 1614, saying that the marriage was not for "affection, but for the good of this plantation, for the honor of our country." She took the name Rebecca Rolfe and sailed to England with him, dying there of a fever in 1617. Their son Thomas returned to Virginia, where he married and had children. Some Virginians today proudly claim Pocahontas as their ancestor.

When this portrait of Pocahontas was made in 1616, she was about twenty-one years old and was to die only a year later. Her real name was Matoaka and her nickname, Pocahontas, means either "playful one" or "my favorite daughter."

THE WESTWARD PUSH

Powhatan died in 1618. The new chief, his brother Opechancanough, did not share his predecessor's welcoming attitude toward the colonists. Angered by the way his people were being pushed off their lands, he led several attacks on the newcomers, killing 350 settlers in just one conflict. In response to the violence, English troops forced even more Indians out of the area and farther west. By the 1650s some colonists were also starting to move west into the Piedmont. The area was harder to farm, but there was a benefit. The abundant running water supplied power to mills, leading to the first factories in the area.

Communication between the settlers in the western part of Virginia and the colony's governing body, the House of Burgesses, was poor. The settlers became frustrated at their lack of a voice in how the colony was run. In 1676 a group of western farmers led by Nathaniel Bacon rebelled against Governor Berkeley. This uprising, known as Bacon's Rebellion, was the first American revolt against British authority. As a result, western Virginia earned more representation in the House of Burgesses.

By the eighteenth century life had become more comfortable for many Virginia settlers, especially those who had profited in the New World. The wealthy sent their sons to the College of William and Mary, the second-oldest college in the United States, in Williamsburg. They often employed tutors for their children. These tutors had to be disciplinarians as much as teachers. One described a typical morning in 1774: "Before Breakfast Nancy & Fanny had a Fight about a Shoe Brush which they both wanted—Fanny pull'd off her Shoe and threw it at Nancy, which missed her and broke a pane of glass of our School Room."

Most people's houses were not as luxurious or as long lasting as the large dwellings that the wealthy owned, many of which have been lovingly

This modern reproduction of the capitol of Colonial Williamsburg is a faithful copy of the original building, which burned to the ground in 1747.

preserved for us to admire today. Thomas Jefferson said that the majority of houses were "very rarely constructed of stone or brick; much the greatest proportion being of scantling [a small piece of lumber] and boards, plastered with lime. It is impossible to devise things more ugly, uncomfortable, and happily more perishable."

WE, THE PEOPLE

From 1754 to 1763, a battle over land rights called the French and Indian War was fought in the colonies. Many Virginians joined the English side fighting against the French and Indians. One of these soldiers was young George Washington. He enjoyed military life, writing: "I heard the bullets

Before he became a general in the colonial army, George Washington served in the Virginia militia. In this portrait by Charles Willson Peale, Washington stares thoughtfully away, as though imagining his future.

whistle, and believe me, there is something charming in the sound." Washington served as an aide to British general Edward Braddock, who did not hold the young colonist in high regard. When rejecting some advice given to him by Washington, Braddock said haughtily, "These are high times when a British general is to take counsel of a Virginia buckskin."

The alliance with the British did not last long. The colonists were growing resentful of the control that England had over their lives. The Stamp Act, which forced the colonists to pay taxes on any official document, enraged them. The final insult came when the king's governor closed the House of Burgesses in 1774. Enraged at this loss of even the little power they had over their own affairs, many Virginians and other colonists as well resolved to form a new country.

Virginians were among the most vocal and persuasive revolutionaries. "I am not a Virginian," said Patrick Henry, "but an American." One year later, Henry made a speech protesting the power the English government held over the colonists' lives, concluding, "Give me liberty, or give me death!"

Virginia's Thomas Jefferson wrote the Declaration of Independence, which announced that the former colonies were now an independent country. England refused to accept this bold statement, and war soon broke out. Although the words and actions of many Virginians had led to the war, very little of it was actually fought on their land. Only the war's last battle and the final surrender of the British took place there, in Yorktown.

The young country needed to draft a constitution, and two Virginians took over much of the task. George Mason had written a large part of Virginia's constitution, and James Madison relied heavily on the document when he was writing the U.S. Constitution, which defined the principles on which the new nation was to be based. Its definition of the country as a union of semi-independent states was unheard of in Europe. Rather it was a system used by several groups of Native Americans, including the Iroquois. Many scholars think that the early framers of the U.S. Constitution were familiar with and admired the Iroquois system, using it as a model when setting up the nation's government.

Before the U.S. Constitution was written, Mason had written the Virginia Declaration of Rights, which would form the basis of the Bill of Rights, the first ten amendments to the Constitution.

As the new nation was taking shape, an older civilization was coming close to being destroyed. Virginia's native people had been dying off ever since the arrival of the European settlers. Many were killed violently in conflicts between the two groups. Others died of diseases introduced by the newcomers. Thomas Jefferson noted a sharp decline in the numbers of Indians in his native state. He estimated that there were only three or four Mattaponi Indians left, between ten and twelve Pamunkey, and no men among the few remaining Nottaway.

"AN INHUMAN PRACTICE"

Africans—twenty of them—first arrived in the colony in 1619, when a Dutch slave ship traded them for food and water. They were indentured servants—once they had worked enough to pay for their passage, they would be free. The same was not true for the first slaves, brought to the colony in the 1640s.

In his *Notes on the State of Virginia,* Thomas Jefferson mentioned that an "inhuman practice once prevailed in this country, of making slaves of the Indians." Oddly, Jefferson did not seem to find the enslavement of Africans and African Americans inhuman—just of Native Americans. Although he said that he did not approve of owning slaves, he never freed his own.

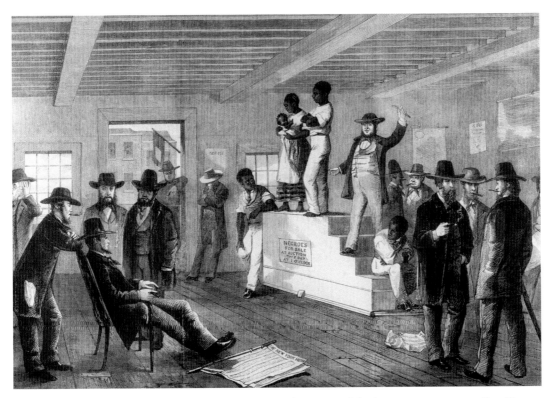

A slave family awaits its fate on a Richmond auction block. In many cases, family members were separated never to see one another again.

Many farmers in Virginia used enslaved people to grow and harvest their crops. Because the overplanting of tobacco had exhausted the soil, farmers needed more workers to make a profit. In the 1790s Virginia had 270,000 slaves and 296,000 free citizens, both black and white. Virginia quickly became an important center for buying and selling slaves. Everyone profited but the slaves, whose lives, never easy, got harder and harder.

A Virginian named Nat Turner thought that God wanted him to organize his fellow slaves to kill white citizens. When a mysterious black spot moved across the face of the sun one day in August 1831, Turner said, "Just as the black spot passed over the sun, so shall the blacks pass over the earth." He led his followers through Southampton County, killing dozens of white men, women, and children. County residents armed themselves and fought back, capturing Turner and killing hundreds of blacks, most of whom had had nothing to do with the rebellion. Turner was executed. His revolt had failed, and whites, fearful of another attack, made life even more difficult for the slaves.

All the while, the slave trade only grew in Virginia. In 1832 more than six thousand slaves were sold there. The tensions brought about by these sales, together with the new restrictions on the lives of African Americans, helped bring about the Civil War.

The more industrialized Northern states had never been as dependent on slave labor as the South, and now abolitionists were calling for an end to slavery. The slaveholders and many people in the North insisted that the individual states, and not the country as a whole, had the right to decide whether or not to abolish slavery. Many other people disagreed, believing that it was a national issue. The debate raged and bitterly divided the country. Then on December 20, 1860, South Carolina seceded, or withdrew, from the Union. In early 1861 five more Southern states seceded as well, and together they formed the Confederate States of America. Eventually five additional states, including Virginia, were to join the Confederacy. The North and South were officially at war.

Unlike the American Revolution, which had mostly bypassed Virginia, the Civil War raged in the state. Of the war's 4,000 battles, 2,200 were fought in Virginia. Thousands of Virginians died. Before the Battle of Gettysburg in Pennsylvania, which was disastrous for the South, General George Pickett encouraged his troops by saying, "Up, men, and to your posts! Don't forget today that you are from Old Virginia." But the fighting did not take place only on land. The first sea battle between ironclad warships occurred at Hampton Roads, Virginia, in 1862 when the *Monitor* and the *Merrimack* fought a bloody fight. The *Merrimack* was eventually seized by the Confederacy and renamed the *Virginia*.

During the Civil War, not only soldiers but also civilians suffered horribly. Richmond, the capital of the Confederacy, was the scene of bread riots in 1863. People desperate for food broke into stores and warehouses, taking everything edible they could lay their hands on. After four punishing years of the worst fighting Americans have ever known, the Confederate troops, under the Virginian Robert E. Lee, surrendered at Appomattox Court House, Virginia.

Frightened city residents flee Richmond on April 2, 1865. Confederate soldiers set fire to a few of the city's warehouses, and soon the flames were out of control. The destruction was only increased by a mob, which helped spread the fire to other parts of town.

People in Virginia have not forgotten the war, even though it ended more than 140 years ago. Re-enactors dress up as soldiers, striving to be as authentic as possible. They stage important battles of the conflict. In addition, every October, the Civil War Weekend is held in Manassas, the site of the war's first major land battle. People dressed in Civil War costumes lead tours, giving the history of the battle.

Dressed in period costumes, these men re-enact the important Civil War battle at Manassas.

"A NOISE, TERRIFIC AS OF CRASHING WORLDS"

Cornelia Peake McDonald lived in Winchester, the scene of much bloody fighting during the Civil War. Her infant daughter died in August 1862 while battles raged around their home. She wrote the following description of what happened next:

After she was buried, I was lying in bed with a feeling only of indifference to everything, a perfect deadness of soul and spirit. If I had a wish it was the world, with its fearful trials and sorrows, its mockeries and its vanishing joys, could come to an end. Suddenly the house was shaken to its foundations, the glass was shivered from the windows and fell like rain all over me as I lay in bed; a noise, terrific as of crashing worlds, followed, prolonged for some fearful moments.

My first thought was that the world was really in its last convulsion. I could not move, but lay fixed and paralyzed. Then a cry, and my room door was burst open. "The town is on fire!" screamed Betty, rushing in. I got up and running across the hall to where the windows looked towards the town, and then saw the whole eastern sky lighted by the blaze of burning buildings, a long line of which was in one huge conflagration. . . . [The Union soldiers'] great magazine [gunpowder warehouse] had been blown up, which had caused the fearful noise. . . . A battle had taken place a short distance off, and many killed on both sides. . . .

My boys in looking over the field for whatever they could find of arms or any thing else left behind in the haste of the fugitives, came across the mutilated remains of the poor creature who had been sent back to see if the fuse was burning. One foot was found in our garden.

ALL QUIET ALONG THE POTOMAC

Virginia saw its share of bloody battles during the Civil War—Bull Run and Richmond among them. But when no fighting broke out on any given day, a familiar War Department announcement published in the nation's newspapers was: "All quiet along the Potomac." One day in September 1861, these words followed the customary headline: "A picket [front-line guard] shot." In the November 30 edition of *Harper's Weekly,* under the title "The Picket Guard," this poem appeared. Within a short time the verses were set to music by various composers, both from the North and from the South.

Words by Mrs. Ethel Lynn Beers   **Music by W. H. Godwin**

"All qui - et a - long the Po - to - mac," they say, Ex - cept now and then a stray pick - et is shot as he walks on his beat to and fro, By a ri - fle - man hid in the thick - et. 'Tis noth - ing, a pri - vate or two now and then Will not count in the news of the bat - tle; Not an of - fi - cer lost, on - ly one of the men, Moan - ing out all a - lone the death rat - tle.

All quiet along the Potomac tonight,
Where the soldiers lie peacefully
   dreaming,
Their tents in the rays of the clear
   autumn moon,
O'er the light of the watch fires, are
   gleaming;
A tremulous sign, as the gentle night
   wind,
Through the forest leaves softly is
   creeping,
While stars up above, with their
   glittering eyes,
Keep guard for the army is sleeping.

There's only the sound of the lone
   sentry's tread,
As he tramps from the rock to the
   fountain,
And he thinks of the two in the low
   trundle bed,
Far away in the cot on the mountain.
His musket falls slack, and his face,
   dark and grim,
Grows gentle with memories tender,
As he mutters a prayer for the children
   asleep,
For their mother, may Heaven defend
   her.

The moon seems to shine just as
   brightly as then,
That night when the love yet unspoken
Leaped up to his lips when low-mur-
   mured vows
Were pledged to be ever unbroken.
Then drawing his sleeve roughly over
   his eyes,
He dashes off tears that are welling,
And gathers his gun closer up to its
   place
As if to keep down the heart-swelling.

He passes the fountain, the blasted
   pine tree,
The footstep is lagging and weary;
Yet onward he goes, through the broad
   belt of light,
Toward the shades of the forest so
   dreary.
Hark! Was it the night wind that
   rustled the leaves?
Was it moonlight so wondrously
   flashing?
It looks like a rifle—"Ah! Mary, good-
   bye!"
And the lifeblood is ebbing and
   splashing.

All quiet along the Potomac tonight,
No sound save the rush of the river;
While soft falls the dew on the face of
   the dead—
[Skip to last beat of fourth from last
   measure]
The picket's off duty forever.

UP FROM SLAVERY

Times were hard throughout the South in the years after the Civil War. During this period, known as Reconstruction, most of the former Confederate states, including Virginia, refused to accept the fourteenth amendment to the U.S. Constitution, which made slavery illegal. So the federal government put these states under military rule. Some northerners, called carpetbaggers after their suitcases made hastily from pieces of carpet sewn together, took advantage of southerners, both black and white. Virginia finally accepted the fourteenth amendment in 1870 and passed a state constitution acceptable to the federal government in Washington, D.C. Virginia was part of the Union again.

The end of slavery did not bring about equality between the races. In many cases former slaves stayed on the plantations where they had been born. They sharecropped, or farmed the land, paying a share of the crop to its owner. Although they were legally free, the sharecroppers were as bound to the land and its white owners as they had been under slavery.

Almost all of the black population was uneducated, since strict laws had forbidden anyone from teaching them to read. Few were trained in useful skills. Some of the first reading lessons to former slaves and other African Americans were given in Virginia under a tree later called the Emancipation Oak. Soon the nation's first mostly black university, Hampton University, was founded in Hampton in 1868. Booker T. Washington, a former slave and Hampton graduate, founded Tuskegee Institute (now Tuskegee University) in Alabama. He wrote an autobiography, called *Up from Slavery*, to inspire other African Americans to get an education and make a difference in their lives and in the world.

Despite these gains in education, the racial divide grew even wider. A new state constitution, adopted in 1902, took the right to vote away from

African-American and Asian-American students attend class at the Hampton Institute in 1899. The institute, now Hampton University, was founded in 1868 to educate former slaves.

black Virginians and called for the separation of the races in schools, transportation, and housing—in short, in nearly every aspect of life. These regulations, which existed throughout the South, were called Jim Crow laws. Blacks suspected of small offenses, such as being rude to a white person, were often lynched—attacked by a mob and killed, usually by hanging. Their bodies were sometimes left in public places to frighten others. About one hundred African Americans were lynched in Virginia between 1880 and 1920.

Most Virginians were horrified by lynching. They elected the dynamic Harry Flood Byrd to the governor's office in 1926, and in 1928 Byrd pushed through laws calling for swift and severe punishment for this crime.

TO THE PRESENT

More than 100,000 Virginians fought in World War I, many of them training at Virginia's Langley Air Force Base. World War II saw even more Virginians in uniform: 300,000. Serving together in uniform led many Virginians to see that they were all the same and helped bring about the end of the cruel Jim Crow laws. Federal courts ordered schools desegregated in 1954. Many Virginians refused to obey this law at first. But finally, in 1959, public schools were integrated.

Many white people still resisted sending their children to schools with black children. To combat this, in 1970 Virginia's governor A. Linwood Holton showed his support for integration by personally taking his white

POPULATION GROWTH: 1790–2000

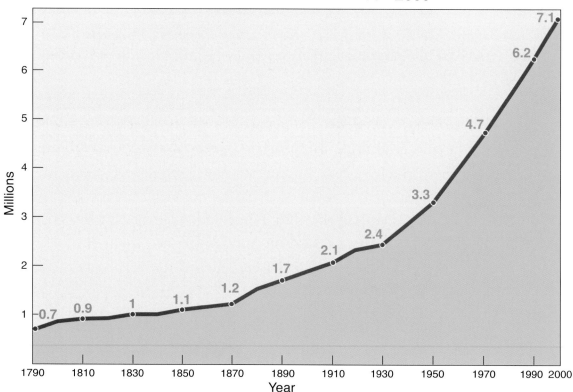

L. Douglas Wilder, Virginia's first African-American governor, waves to a crowd.

child to a mostly black school in Richmond. Inspired by his example, other white people began to do the same. Lara Semones grew up in the town of Radford and attended the small high school there. She says, "I went to a high school that was almost exactly half black and half white, and the first time I noticed racial tensions was after I left there. We got along quite well." She recalls with pride her small town's valiant efforts to keep members of the racist organization the Ku Klux Klan from marching through Radford.

The people who overcame the "starving time"—the Revolution, the Civil War, and Reconstruction—are working to defeat this enemy, racism, as well. A major step toward this end was taken in 1990, when L. Douglas Wilder was sworn in as the first elected African-American governor in the United States.

Chapter Three

"Plain, Honest . . . Neighbors"

Thomas Jefferson wrote of Virginia, "This country . . . consists of plain, honest, and rational neighbors . . . hospitable and friendly." While that was—and still is—true of many Virginians, not everyone would agree with him. The Native Americans, for example, whose lands were taken from them, might disagree. Indians used to be free to live and hunt throughout what became the entire state of Virginia. Now only two tiny parts of the state remain in their control. The Pamunkey, once the largest group of the Powhatan Confederacy, live on a small, 800-acre reservation, while the Mattaponi survive on merely 125 acres.

As long ago as 1609, some European settlers objected to the theft of these lands. In that year Reverend Robert Gray asked his congregation, "By what right or warrant can we enter into the land of these Savages, take away their rightfull inheritance from them, and plant ourselves in their places, being unwronged or unprovoked by them?" But few shared his point of

Virginia is home to people of many religious traditions, including these Mennonite women who admire the view at Ravens Roost Overlook on the scenic Blue Ridge Parkway.

view, and the settlers continued to push the Native Americans off their land. Today less than 1 percent of the state's population claims Indian ancestry.

BLACK AND WHITE IN VIRGINIA

Relations between blacks and whites have not always been pleasant. Although Jim Crow laws and the era of lynching are in the past, racial division is still strong in the state. Despite the fact that segregation is illegal, many children still attend schools made up almost entirely of children of their own race.

Many officials and residents in Virginia are working to improve relations between the races. Each January Lee-Jackson Day honors Confederate generals Robert E. Lee and Thomas "Stonewall" Jackson and another holiday honors civil-rights leader Martin Luther King Jr., all of whom were born in January. Statues of Lee and Jackson stand on Richmond's Monument Avenue. The celebration of only their birthdays sparked anger in the black community, though, so Dr. King's memorial was added to honor an African-American hero too. In 1996 a statue of Arthur Ashe, African-American tennis great and AIDS activist, was unveiled.

In 2003 Virginia Beach was found to be the most racially integrated city in the United States with regard to whites and African Americans. There is still a difference between the cities and the country, however. Susan McArthur moved to the rural part of the Piedmont. She says that in the country, unlike the cities, there is a strict division between the races. She points out, "The underclass is black and, because it's rural and agricultural, they're very poor and relatively uneducated. We don't have a middle-class black population in the farming areas."

The whites in Virginia come from many different lands. The early population of Virginia was mostly English, with some Irish, Scottish,

A mother and her two children take advantage of the mild weather in Christiansburg to read a book on the front steps of their home.

Welsh, French, and German as well. This mix has changed through the centuries. Today around 70 percent of the state's population is of European heritage, tracing their ancestors mostly to Great Britain and Germany. About one-fifth of Virginians are black, and this proportion is expected

ETHNIC VIRGINIA

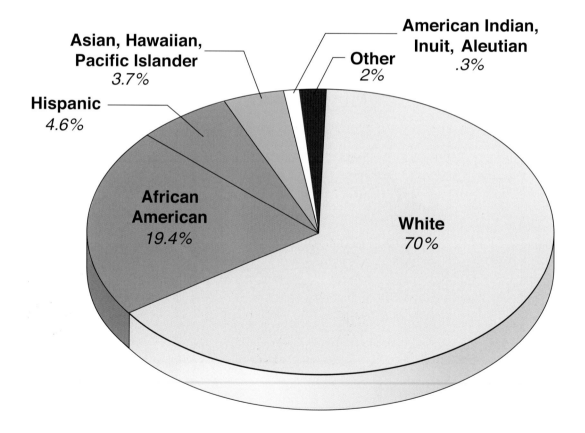

American Indian,
Inuit, Aleutian
.3%

Other
2%

Asian, Hawaiian,
Pacific Islander
3.7%

Hispanic
4.6%

African
American
19.4%

White
70%

More and more immigrants are transforming the face of Virginia. The three women on the right have come to America from Vietnam. They are learning how to shop in their new homeland.

THE FOXHUNT

Sally Goldfarb grew up foxhunting. She belonged to the Pony Club, an international organization for children who like to ride horses. Many of Virginia's Pony Clubs are linked to local hunt groups. The children are supposed to ride in the back of the field so they do not get in the way of the more experienced riders, but Sally says, "My pony loved to hunt and I would often be seen hunting in the front of the field."

The rider who leads the hunters is called the Master. The Huntsman cares for the foxhounds, Virginia's state dog. He or she is familiar with the behavior of the hounds and can recognize from their barks and howls when they have found a fox. He blows a signal on a horn to alert the other hunters. Then there is an exciting chase across country, with hounds and horses leaping over fences and hedges, wading across streams, and galloping over fields. If the hounds get distracted by the scent of another animal, such as a deer, the Whipper-In cracks a whip in the air. The loud sound reminds the dogs that they are in the business of hunting a fox, not a deer, and they usually return to their task. When the fox "goes to ground"—down its hole—the hounds are called back and the fox is left to recover from a hard day.

to rise. About 260,000 are Asian, and 193,000 are Hispanic. American Indians number about 15,000, or less than 1 percent of the population.

Some of these ethnic groups enjoy special festivals. The capital city of Richmond hosts many ethnic fairs. Kapanga Kasongo, originally from the Congo, particularly enjoys October, when different groups are honored. In that month Richmond hosts an African fair, an Italian-themed Columbus Day festival, and Oktoberfest, celebrating Germany. "There's always something going on," Kasongo says.

SCOTLAND IN VIRGINIA

The first Scots came to Virginia as indentured servants. More Scots came in the eighteenth century, when many of them unsuccessfully supported their king James's claim to the throne of England. Some of the rebels who were caught were sent as prisoners to the penal colony of Carolina and Virginia. Still others were sent to the colonies to ease overcrowding at home. Most of them were bankers, tradespeople, and merchants involved in the import/export trade.

Alexandria was founded as a trading post by Scots. Dumfries, Fredericksburg, and Petersburg all had many Scots as their founders. The Shenandoah Valley originally was opened up and farmed by Scotch-Irish and German immigrants.

Today many Virginians enjoy celebrating their Scottish past. Virginia is home to the second-largest Scottish festival in the United States, the Virginia Scottish Games and Gathering of the Clans, held every July in Alexandria. As many as 200,000 people attend this festival each year, many of them wearing traditional Scottish clothes. They eat Scottish food, play traditional Scottish games, compete in country dancing, and enjoy the music of the bagpipes.

Many of Virginia's residents take pride in their Scottish heritage. The groom in this wedding in Onancock wears a traditional kilt and long socks.

CHOCOLATE CHESS PIE

No one knows for sure where the name *chess pie* comes from. One explanation is that it does not have any special ingredients, so it is not apple pie, peach pie, or pumpkin pie—it is "jes' pie." Whatever the origin of the name, chess pie is a southern favorite, and this variation with chocolate won the blue ribbon at the Virginia State Fair for Pat Heath of New Kent.

Yield: 6 to 8 servings
2 cups sugar
2 tablespoons cornstarch
4 eggs
1 can (8 oz.) chocolate-flavored syrup
1/4 cup milk
1/4 cup butter, melted
1 unbaked pie shell

Ask an adult to help you combine the sugar, cornstarch, eggs, chocolate-flavored syrup, milk, and butter in a bowl. Beat until smooth, using an electric mixer at medium speed. Pour into an unbaked pie shell. Bake in a 350° F oven for 55 minutes or until the center is set. Cool on a rack, then slice, serve, and enjoy.

RICHMOND'S JEWISH HERITAGE

Richmond is home to the sixth-oldest synagogue in the United States. In the eighteenth century the then-small city had 2,500 free people—slaves were not counted—including a Jewish population of about 100. This was a larger percentage than either New York or Philadelphia had at that time. Today about 66,000 Virginians, or a little less than 1 percent of the state's population, are Jewish.

The Jewish cemetery of Beth Shalome was first used in 1791. Its founders underestimated the size of the population that would use it, and by 1816 it was already full, so the new Hebrew Cemetery was opened nearby.

For the most part, the Jewish population in Richmond led lives quite similar to those of their non-Jewish neighbors. They owned slaves, although some objected to the practice. They participated in the economic fortunes of the city. Their young men went off to fight in the Confederate Army, and those who were killed were buried in the world's only Jewish military cemetery outside of Israel.

Today Richmond's Church Hill is the home of Kenesseth Israel synagogue, founded in 1856. A large percentage of the city's Jewish population still lives in that neighborhood, where their ancestors lived and worshiped before them. Nearby the Beth Ahabah Museum and Archives, containing documents and other materials related to the lives of Richmond's Jewish community, is open to the public.

REGIONAL LIVES

The people of western Virginia have traditionally been an independent group. The west has felt isolated since the days of Nathaniel Bacon's 1676 rebellion against the House of Burgesses. They did not always take kindly to submitting to the state's rules. An early settler in the west, Adam O'Brien, said he hated "those varmints, the sheriffs and constables." He said that earlier settlers had "lived quite happy before the Revolution, for then there was no law, no courts and no sheriffs [but] then came the lawyers and next the preachers, and from that time they never had any peace anymore."

In the Piedmont, country life resembles life in nineteenth-century England, says Susan McArthur. The wealthier people live in beautiful

People who live in rural areas, like this family in Craig County, are linked by computer to other state residents, thanks to "electronic villages" set up by Virginia State University.

DRY FRYE: A VIRGINIA FOLKTALE

There once was an old man named Dry Frye. . . . And one time he stayed for supper, and he was eatin' fried chicken so fast, he got a chicken bone stuck in his throat. Choked him to death. Well, the man of the house he was scared. "Law me!" he says, "they'll find old Dry Frye here, and they'll hang me for murder sure!" So he took old Dry Frye to a house down the road a piece and propped him up against the door. Somebody went to go out the door, and directly old Dry Frye fell in the house. "Law me!" says the man of the house. "Hit's old Dry Frye!" (Everybody knew old Dry Frye.) "We got to get shet of him quick or we're liable to be hung for murder!"

So he took old Dry Frye and propped him up in the bresh 'side the road. And way up in the night some men come along, thought it was a highway robber layin' for 'em. So they chunked rocks at him, knocked him down, and when they seen who it was (everybody knew old Dry Frye), they thought they'd killed him, and they got scared they'd be hung for murder. . . .

Well, they took old Dry Frye and propped him up against a man's corn house. And that man he went out early the next mornin'; and he's been missin' corn—so when he seen there was somebody over there at his corn house, he ran and got his gun. Slipped around, hollered, "Get away from there or I'll shoot!"

old houses and have servants. Many of them send their children to boarding schools. She says, "In other parts of the country, people judge you by your education, your job, even your income. Here, the important thing to find out is 'What's your family name? How long have you been here?'" Even the countryside looks like England.

Politically the citizens of the Tidewater and Piedmont areas are more liberal than those of the west. It has been said that the

And when old Dry Frye never moved, he shot, and Dry Frye tumbled over and hit the ground.

"Law me!" says the man. "I believe that was old Dry Frye." (Everybody knew Dry Frye.) "Now I've done killed him and I'll sure get hung for murder."

[Dry Fry has more misadventures, until he is found by an old woman and her family.]

Well, they had some wild horses in a wilderness out on the mountain. So they rounded up one of 'em, put him in the barn. Then they put an old no-'count saddle on him and an old piece of bridle, and put old Dry Frye on . . . and opened . . . the barn door and let the horse go. He shot out of there, and down the road he went with that old preacher-man a-bouncin' first one side and then the other. And them rogues run out and went to shootin' and hollerin', "He's stole our horse! Stop him! Somebody stop him yonder! Horse thief! Horse thief!"

Everybody down the road come runnin' out their houses a-shoutin' and hollerin' and a-shootin' around, but that horse had done jumped the fence and took out up the mountain, and it looked like he was headed for Kentucky.

And as far as I know, old Dry Frye is over there yet, a-tearin' around through the wilderness on that wild horse.

Appalachians form a "great spine of Republicanism which runs down the back of the [mostly Democratic] South."

Today many of the barriers between the east and the west have been removed. Differences still exist, however. Ethel-Marie Underhill lives near Roanoke, in southwestern Virginia. She says, "I moved here from Kansas and found it harder to get acquainted with local people since they're more reserved than midwesterners." Susan McArthur

Bales of hay are piled beside a barn. In the twenty-first century, barriers between rural and urban Virginia are slowly being erased. Still, remote communities and country living are a key part of the state's identity.

shares her opinion, saying, "After thirty years, I still feel like an outsider because I wasn't born here."

Lara Semones agrees, but adds that ultimately the residents of small, tightly knit towns tend to help out one another. "On the other hand, you have a community that really cares about each other and wants to help each other. People help out when there's a death in the family or illness."

POPULATION
DISTRIBUTION

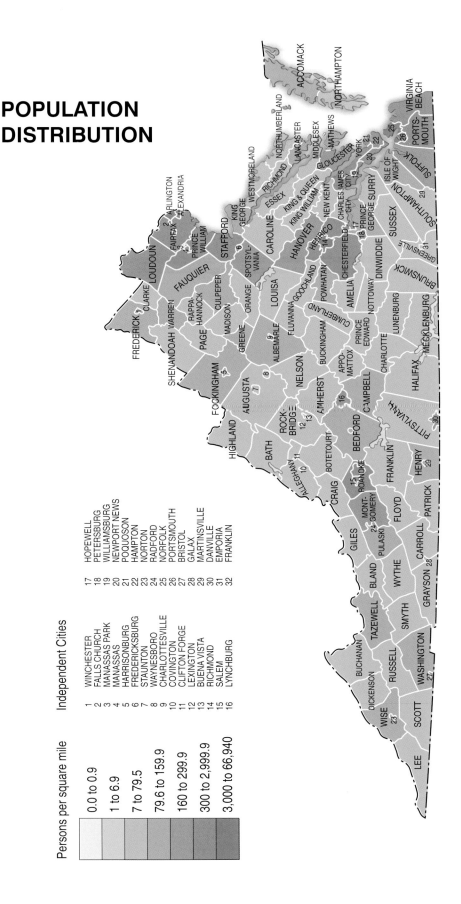

Persons per square mile

0.0 to 0.9

1 to 6.9

7 to 79.5

79.6 to 159.9

160 to 299.9

300 to 2,999.9

3,000 to 66,940

Independent Cities

1	WINCHESTER
2	FALLS CHURCH
3	MANASSAS PARK
4	MANASSAS
5	HARRISONBURG
6	FREDERICKSBURG
7	STAUNTON
8	WAYNESBORO
9	CHARLOTTESVILLE
10	COVINGTON
11	CLIFTON FORGE
12	LEXINGTON
13	BUENA VISTA
14	RICHMOND
15	SALEM
16	LYNCHBURG
17	HOPEWELL
18	PETERSBURG
19	WILLIAMSBURG
20	NEWPORT NEWS
21	POQUOSON
22	HAMPTON
23	NORTON
24	RADFORD
25	NORFOLK
26	PORTSMOUTH
27	BRISTOL
28	GALAX
29	MARTINSVILLE
30	DANVILLE
31	EMPORIA
32	FRANKLIN

The graves of unknown soldiers in Winchester's Confederate cemetery are a powerful reminder of the state's strong southern heritage.

Northern Virginians sometimes feel even more isolated. Most of that part of the state is made up of the suburbs of Washington, D.C., and the residents have more in common with the northern United States than with the rest of their state. Sally Goldfarb of Winchester says, "I never felt southern." But her husband decided to prove to her that Virginia is part of the south. He showed her the Confederate flag in Winchester's town square. Finally, a visit to Winchester's Confederate graveyard was enough to convince her that the city indeed had a strong southern heritage.

Lara Semones, on the other hand, is from the southern part of Virginia and has always felt like a real southerner. She is upset by the prejudices many people in other parts of the United States have against southerners and says, "When I moved up north I was labeled as being unintelligent, super-conservative, and racist because I was from the South. I felt like an ambassador and was constantly defending the South."

In the end, Virginia stands for many things, and throughout its history it has drawn people from different races and faiths to settle together peaceably and call it home.

Chapter Four

Governing the Old Dominion

The part of Virginia closest to Washington, D.C., is home to more than 2 million people. About a quarter of them work for the U.S. government. You might think that with so many Virginians spending all their days working for the federal government, they would have little interest in how their own state is run. But this is not the case. Virginians are constantly changing laws and making new ones. As recently as 1970, Virginia adopted a totally new state constitution.

Virginia currently sends eleven representatives and two senators to the U.S. Congress. In 2003 three representatives were Democrats and eight were Republicans, while both senators were Republicans.

INSIDE GOVERNMENT

Like the federal, or national, system, Virginia has three branches of government: the legislative, the executive, and the judicial.

Thomas Jefferson designed Virginia's capitol building, which was built between 1785 and 1792. Two wings were added between 1904 and 1906.

Legislative

In 1619 the citizens of Virginia formed a legislative body called the House of Burgesses. The present-day state assembly is the direct descendant of that governing body, making it the oldest group of elected officials in the United States.

The state assembly is divided into two parts, the senate (with forty members serving four-year terms) and the house of delegates (made up of one hundred members serving two-year terms). The leader of each of the divisions is elected by the other members. The assembly makes the state laws, decides the amount of taxes people and corporations must pay, and approves how the state's money is to be spent. Since the state has so many expenses, the legislature decided to earn more money for education through a state lottery. In 2002 the lottery added $368 million to the state's treasury.

Executive

This branch consists of three elected officials and a number of appointed officials. The governor, the head of the executive branch, along with the lieutenant governor and the attorney general are each elected.

Virginia's governor serves for four years per term and may not serve more than two terms in a row. He or she performs many important jobs for the state. The governor is the commander-in-chief of the state militia and police force. The governor also enforces the laws and prepares the state's budget, or spending plan. Like many other states, Virginia has a law that says the state must have a balanced budget, spending no more money in any year than it takes in through taxes and other earnings. The governor may veto, or reject, any laws passed by the assembly. But if two-thirds of the members of the assembly vote to overturn the veto, the law can still be passed.

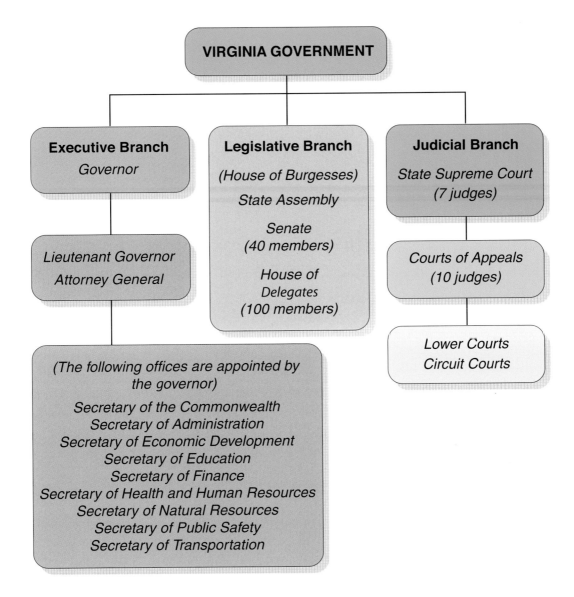

VIRGINIA GOVERNMENT

Executive Branch
Governor

Lieutenant Governor
Attorney General

(The following offices are appointed by the governor)
Secretary of the Commonwealth
Secretary of Administration
Secretary of Economic Development
Secretary of Education
Secretary of Finance
Secretary of Health and Human Resources
Secretary of Natural Resources
Secretary of Public Safety
Secretary of Transportation

Legislative Branch
(House of Burgesses)
State Assembly
Senate
(40 members)
House of Delegates
(100 members)

Judicial Branch
State Supreme Court
(7 judges)
Courts of Appeals
(10 judges)
Lower Courts
Circuit Courts

The lieutenant governor helps the governor and also takes over the governor's job if the governor dies or becomes too sick to govern. The attorney general is the chief legal advisor to the governor and often works with members of the judicial branch.

Judicial

This branch is made up of the state's court system. The courts interpret the laws written by the assembly and decide the outcome of legal cases. The most important court, the state supreme court, consists of seven justices, whose leader is called the chief justice. The justices serve twelve-year terms. Lower courts include the court of appeals, the thirty-one circuit courts, district courts, and many juvenile and domestic-relations courts.

"MOTHER OF PRESIDENTS"

Eight American presidents were born in Virginia, more than in any other state. This includes four of the first five: George Washington (president 1789–1797), Thomas Jefferson (1801–1809), James Madison (1809–1817), and James Monroe (1817–1825). The other four are William Henry Harrison (1841), John Tyler (1841–1845), Zachary Taylor (1849–1850), and Woodrow Wilson (1913–1921).

Not only presidents, but other national politicians have come from Virginia. Patrick Henry (1736–1799), the patriot whose brilliant speeches put into words what so many colonists were thinking about winning their independence from England, was a member of the House of Burgesses. He also served a term as Virginia's governor.

Many members of the First Continental Congress, whose members decided that the colonies had to become free of England, were Virginians. Among them was the Continental Congress's first president, Peyton Randolph (1721–1775).

John Marshall (1755–1835) started his career in local Virginia politics and became chief justice of the United States in 1801. Marshall helped make the Supreme Court the highly respected legal body it is today.

John Tyler became president in 1841 when President William Henry Harrison died after only one month in office.

VIRGINIA BY COUNTY

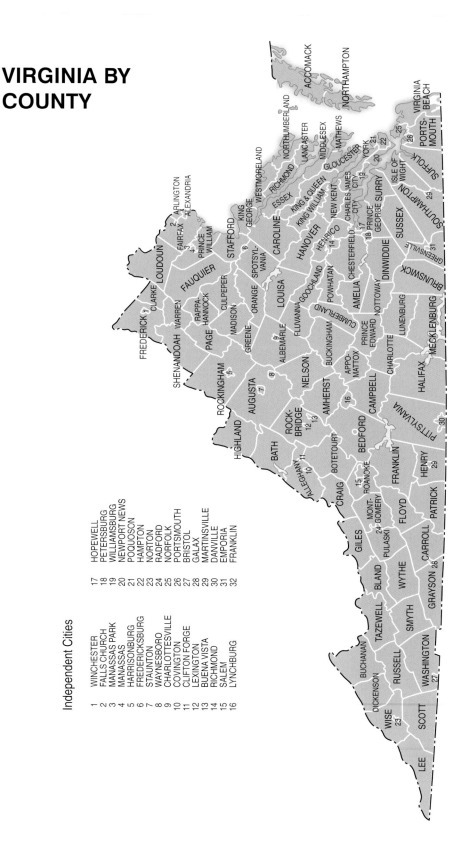

Independent Cities

1	WINCHESTER
2	FALLS CHURCH
3	MANASSAS PARK
4	MANASSAS
5	HARRISONBURG
6	FREDERICKSBURG
7	STAUNTON
8	WAYNESBORO
9	CHARLOTTESVILLE
10	COVINGTON
11	CLIFTON FORGE
12	LEXINGTON
13	BUENA VISTA
14	RICHMOND
15	SALEM
16	LYNCHBURG
17	HOPEWELL
18	PETERSBURG
19	WILLIAMSBURG
20	NEWPORT NEWS
21	POQUOSON
22	HAMPTON
23	NORTON
24	RADFORD
25	NORFOLK
26	PORTSMOUTH
27	BRISTOL
28	GALAX
29	MARTINSVILLE
30	DANVILLE
31	EMPORIA
32	FRANKLIN

In more recent times Virginian George Catlett Marshall (1880–1959) served as the chief of staff of the U.S. Army, secretary of state, and secretary of defense. He is most famous as the author of the European Recovery Plan, usually known as the Marshall Plan. This plan was used to rebuild Europe after World War II and won him the Nobel Peace Prize in 1953.

L. Douglas Wilder was elected governor of Virginia in 1989. The grandson of a slave, Wilder achieved many firsts. He was the first black person in the Virginia senate since Reconstruction, the first black lieutenant governor of Virginia, and the first elected black governor of any state in the United States.

Virginia's John W. Warner served as secretary of the Navy from 1972 to 1974. He has been a U.S. senator since 1979, making him the third-longest-serving senator from Virginia in U.S. history.

SPEAKING OUT ABOUT SCHOOLS

In most school districts, a school board makes the key decisions, including which textbooks will be used, who will serve as principal, and how long the school year will be. Until recently Virginia was the only state in which the members of the school board were appointed by judges or other officials. That has now changed with the passing of a law saying that the people who live in the school district should elect the school board members. Ethel-Marie Underhill, who lives near Roanoke, thinks that this has made a big difference in education. "I'm pleased that school boards are now elected in Virginia," she says, "like all other states. It's nice to have public input."

Kapanga Kasongo, a professor at the University of Richmond, lives near that city. He says that the schools in Richmond do not have as much money to spend on education as the schools in the nearby counties. He says that the county schools "are among the best in the country." He adds,

Education is a top concern in Virginia. Here, students and their teacher work out a problem together.

"A lot of people are moving away from the city of Richmond, and more and more people are moving ten, twenty, thirty miles from the city. It puts enormous financial pressure on the city. Comes the morning everybody flocks to Richmond, but they don't pay taxes there."

The schools are supported by local taxes, so if people who work in Richmond do not actually live there, their tax money goes to support schools in the suburbs and more rural communities. Meanwhile, they are still using the city's resources, such as the streets, the libraries, and the museums. Richmond's concerned parents and educators are looking for ways to correct this imbalance so the city's children can have the best possible education.

CONCERNED ABOUT CRIME

Virginia deals harshly with criminals. It has the death penalty, and since 1976 the state has executed eighty-nine convicted felons, more than any other state except Texas.

Children too can suffer severe criminal punishments in Virginia. Some legislators are concerned with the number of crimes committed by young people. In 1996 the assembly passed laws that reformed the juvenile justice system. Under these reforms, anyone aged fourteen or over who is charged with a serious crime, such as murder or rape, must be punished as an adult. If convicted, the child receives the same punishment as an adult who committed the same crime, and goes to an adult jail. This law makes it easier for school systems to send disruptive children to an alternative school. The reforms also require that children must be tested for emotional problems when they are very young, so that those who need help can start being treated sooner. Virginia's attorney general Jim Gilmore called this a "balanced package" of laws.

An officer takes questions from a group of students who have just toured a helicopter used for law enforcement. Virginia's police force works hard to keep the peace and establish good relations with all of the state's citizens.

Some people say this law could actually increase the amount of juvenile crime. Some young people, particularly those in gangs, are proud of going to jail. The threat of a long jail term may not prevent some of them from committing a crime. Attorney General Gilmore argued that unless something was done to slow down the number of crimes committed by young people, Virginia would see "more rape victims, more murder victims, more funerals, more graves. The time has come to prevent them from hurting other people." Time will tell which opinion proves to be the right one.

The different regions of Virginia have varying rates of crime. For example, although the state as a whole has a relatively low crime rate, Richmond's murder rate usually ranks third or fourth of all the nation's cities. The city is working hard to change that fact. Neighboring counties have lent additional police officers to the city, and the police chief is trying new ideas and programs such as community policing. Officers are also given smaller areas to patrol, so they have time to get to know residents and build good relationships with them.

Chapter Five

Making a Living

As long ago as 1863, the writer Henry David Thoreau expressed disgust at Virginia's dependence on the sale of human beings and tobacco, saying, "What shall a state like Virginia say for itself at the last day, in which these have been the principal, the staple productions? What ground is there for patriotism in such a State?"

The end of slavery brought an end to the era when Virginia relied on trade in human beings for its economic well-being. Tobacco farming, however, is still a source of both income and argument in the state. Each year Virginia makes almost $200 million from its tobacco sales, more than from any other crop. Farmers earn thirty-eight times as much money per acre from tobacco as from wheat. So each time the federal government proposes to raise the sales tax on cigarettes, Virginia's tobacco farmers try to convince their congressional representatives to oppose this increase.

A CHANGING ECONOMY

The workers in Virginia are less dependent on tobacco than they were in the colonial era, though. Other crops are gaining in importance,

A farmer inspects his crop of spring wheat. The grain is an important one in Virginia. About 250,000 acres are devoted to its cultivation.

A farmer examines his tobacco crop.

especially grains, corn, soybeans, and peanuts. Raising poultry and cattle is another valuable part of the state's agriculture industry. Farming in general provides only about 1 percent of the state's annual income. Manufacturing, especially of chemicals, processed foods, cloth, yarn, paper, plastics, and cigarettes, provides most jobs for Virginians.

During the two world wars, manufacturing blossomed in Virginia as large shipyards were started there to make boats for the war effort. Today the Newport News Shipbuilding and Dry Dock Company is the largest privately owned shipyard in the world. Huge ships pull into the docks for repairs, and new ships are built and launched there as well.

2003 GROSS STATE PRODUCT: $304 BILLION

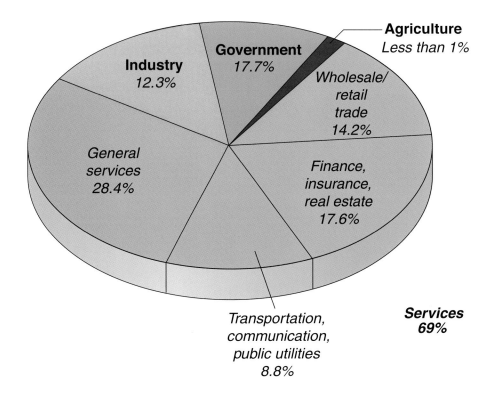

Industry 12.3%
Government 17.7%
Agriculture Less than 1%
Wholesale/retail trade 14.2%
General services 28.4%
Finance, insurance, real estate 17.6%
Transportation, communication, public utilities 8.8%
Services 69%

Farm Wife

Ellen Bryant Voigt was born and raised in Virginia and now lives in Vermont. In this poem, she talks about the hard life of a country woman who imagines flying above all the work and difficulty of her life.

Farm Wife

Dark as the spring river, the earth
opens each damp row as the farmer
swings the far side of the field.
The blackbirds flash their red
wing patches and wheel in his wake,
down to the black dirt; the windmill
grinds in its chain rig and tower.

In the kitchen, his wife is baking.
She stands in the door in her long white
gloves of flour. She cocks her head and
tries to remember, turns like the moon
toward the sea-black field. Her belly
is rising, her apron fills like a sail.
She is gliding now, the windmill churns
beneath her, she passes the farmer,
the fine map of the furrows.
The neighbors point to the bone-white
spot in the sky.

Let her float
like a fat gull that swoops and circles,
before her husband comes in for supper,
before her children grow up and leave her,
before the pulley cranks her down
the dark shaft, and the church blesses
her stone bed, and the earth seals
its black mouth like a scar.

Furniture and clothing factories also have operations in the state. More recently high-tech silicon-producing industries have moved there. Northern Virginia has more than one thousand computer communication companies. Today about 450,000 Virginians work in manufacturing.

The great numbers of people who live in northern Virginia are always in need of new homes, schools, and businesses. All of this building accounts in part for the size of the state's construction industry, which employs roughly 200,000 Virginians. Still others in this part of the state work for the federal government, both in their home state and in nearby Washington, D.C. The Pentagon, which houses the federal government's defense activities, is

The Pentagon houses the U.S. Department of Defense. The building was damaged, and 184 people were killed there, during the September 11, 2001, attacks against the United States.

EARNING A LIVING

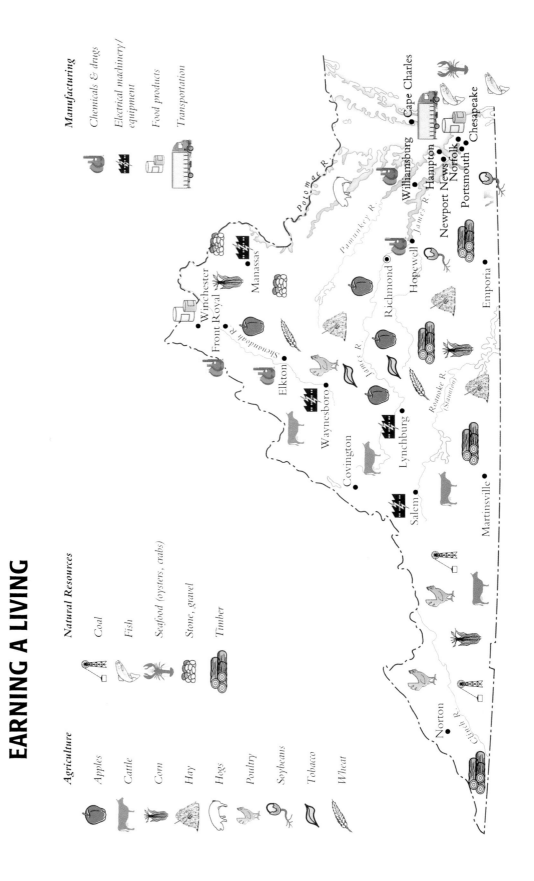

Agriculture

Apples
Cattle
Corn
Hay
Hogs
Poultry
Soybeans
Tobacco
Wheat

Natural Resources

Coal
Fish
Seafood (oysters, crabs)
Stone, gravel
Timber

Manufacturing

Chemicals & drugs
Electrical machinery/ equipment
Food products
Transportation

Night settles on a ship docked at the Norfolk Naval Base.

located in Virginia. So is the Norfolk Naval Base, the largest in the world. The U.S. Marines, Air Force, and Coast Guard all have major installations in the state as well, making the military an important employer.

Tourists spend a lot of money in Virginia. In fact, tourism is the state's third-largest employer. In 2001 tourists spent more than $12.9 billion in the state. More than 210,000 Virginians have jobs in tourism, introducing travelers to the wonders of their state.

A Virginian's average pay in 2000 was $31,120, placing the state twelfth in the nation overall. Still, many Virginians live at or below the poverty line of $18,100 per year. Although the number of people living in poverty in Virginia fell from 12 percent to 10 percent between 1980 and 2002, it is still a problem the state faces. The percentage of unemployed people also dropped, from a high of 8 percent in 1982 to its lowest rate ever of 2.1 percent in 2000. In early 2003 the unemployment rate was up again, to 4.1 percent. According to a 2002 article in the *Roanoke Times,* the gap between rich and poor is growing wider in the state as Virginians are forced to face the shifting fortunes of uncertain economic times.

Another change Virginians have had to face is a shift in the kinds of jobs available in the state. Today some traditional ways of earning a living are all but disappearing. Fishing, for example, has always employed many people in the state. But the increase in manufacturing, while it has created jobs in the state, has polluted the bay and other

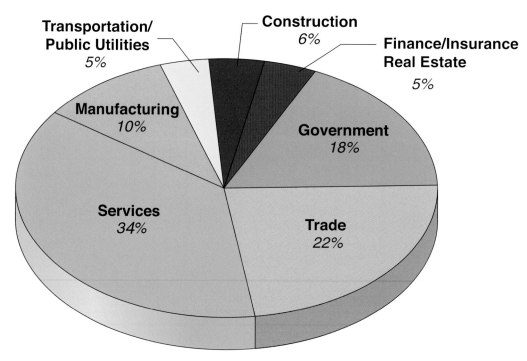

VIRGINIA WORKFORCE

Middle school students learn about the inner workings of a photocopier during a factory tour in York County.

Train cars loaded with coal line up at a rail yard in Norfolk. Though the industry is not as important as it once was to Virginia's economy, workers still unlock the valuable minerals found deep beneath their state.

coastal areas. This pollution has killed many shellfish in the water, forcing many people whose families had fished for generations to look for other sources of income.

Along with the rest of the country, Virginia has developed many jobs in high-tech industries. In 1999 the state ranked third for the number of people employed in this sector.

MINERAL WEALTH

Coal used to be a popular source of energy both for home heating and for fueling machinery. Gradually other forms of energy, especially petroleum, became more important, and America's dependence on coal decreased. In 1970 Virginia produced 35 million tons of coal. A few years later, however, a worldwide oil shortage forced Americans to turn to other sources of energy. Suddenly the coal fields in Virginia grew in importance again. Mining, an industry that had always provided work for some Virginians, employed more and more people. Coal production climbed steadily to a peak of 47 million tons in 1990.

Since then, as the oil supply has become more stable and many scientists are searching for other forms of energy—such as solar and wind—the coal-mining business is once again experiencing a slowdown. Production in 1993 dropped to 39 million tons and has declined steadily ever since.

The people of Virginia have had to alter the ways they earn a living several times in the state's history. They are used to adapting to changing times, continuing to make good use of the state's strong manufacturing and technology industries. Whatever new directions Virginians are faced with, they will continue to work together to meet the challenges of the future.

Chapter Six

Exploring Virginia

Virginia's natural beauty, historic importance, and location make it a fascinating and exciting place to visit. Tourists bring in a lot of money and are a welcome presence, but Virginians are protective of their state. When the Walt Disney Company wanted to locate a theme park in northern Virginia, residents blocked its construction, saying that it would damage the environment and ruin the historical nature of the area.

About 750,000 tourists from all over the world visit Virginia each year. Let's take a minitour ourselves, starting on the Eastern Shore and working our way to the mountains of the west.

THE EASTERN SHORE

The Eastern Shore can be reached from the mainland by the 23-mile Chesapeake Bay Bridge-Tunnel. This is the longest combination bridge and tunnel in the world, and it runs from Norfolk to the southern tip of the peninsula. You can pause along the bridge to watch seagulls from a special pier, to fish, to shop for souvenirs, or to look through the telescopes mounted at the observation areas.

Only a skilled kayaker would dare the rapids at Great Falls on the Potomac River.

PONY PENNING WEEK

Assateague is the largest island off Virginia's Eastern Shore, but no people live there. It is a wildlife refuge inhabited by birds, small mammals, and wild ponies.

No one knows how the ponies got to Assateague. They are similar to horses found on the Outer Banks of the Carolinas and to the mustang, which descended from Spanish horses. They all share certain characteristics, including having one fewer vertebrae (bones of the spinal column) than standard horses. So the ponies are most likely of Spanish origin. How did they get to the island, though?

It is possible that the ancestors of the Assateague ponies escaped from early Spanish explorers. But some people think that they are the descendants of horses that were blinded so they would not be too frightened to work in the gold mines the Spanish hoped to find in the Americas. One theory states that a ship carrying nine ponies was wrecked off the Eastern Shore sometime in the late sixteenth or early seventeenth century, and it is possible that some of them swam

to the island. They then would have interbred with the descendants of horses brought to the island by the British in the 1600s.

For most of the year the ponies live peacefully, disturbed only by an occasional human visitor. But once a year, during the last week of July, called Pony Penning Week locally, many of the ponies are rounded up and made to swim across the narrow channel to Chincoteague Island. There the foals are auctioned off. The money raised benefits the Chincoteague Fire Department, which owns the herd. About 50,000 people, both locals and tourists, go to see the small horses and to bid on them. The horses that are not sold swim back to Assateague.

Some animal rights activists object to this tradition. They say that the animals are unaccustomed to humans and are terrified at being made to swim, which is not a natural activity for horses. But supporters of Pony Penning Week point out that if the ponies are allowed to reproduce without any kind of control, there will soon be too many of them for Assateague to support. By removing some of the ponies, they say, all of them will be healthier.

Once on the Eastern Shore, nature is the biggest attraction. Assateague Island can be reached by bridge from Chincoteague. Much of its wildlife refuge is off-limits to the general public for most of the year, but there is still a lot to see.

The streets of tiny Tangier Island, off the Eastern Shore, are so narrow that cars cannot even fit down them. The island's eight hundred residents get around mainly by bicycle. Most of the inhabitants—originally from Cornwall, England—make their living by fishing. Charming old Victorian houses are another hallmark of the island, which has been isolated through the centuries. In fact, until recently the inhabitants had so little contact with the outside world that they spoke in seventeenth-century English!

Back on the mainland, the small towns along the coast of the peninsula offer their own unique charms. They are known for their beautiful scenery, seafood restaurants, and shops selling local arts and crafts.

THE TIDEWATER

Together Williamsburg, Jamestown, and Yorktown make up what is known as the Historic Triangle, an area that draws tourists and history buffs from all around. Of the three spots, Williamsburg is the most popular. In the 1920s the millionaire John D. Rockefeller became interested in this historic site, which at the time had fallen into disrepair. He founded an organization dedicated to restoring much of the town to its original form, so it could be used in teaching American history. Now eighty-eight buildings have been returned to their original appearance. These include private homes, the governor's mansion, stores, and inns. Guides, some of them children, wear colonial costumes. They lead tourists through the reconstructed section, talking about the history of the

Re-enactors in Colonial Williamsburg march down Duke of Gloucester Street to the accompaniment of a fife-and-drum corps.

Virginia Colony. Hands-on crafts demonstrations teach visitors how to make soap, candles, pots, and other materials using colonial technology. Colonial Williamsburg is also an important source of information about the lives of slaves and free blacks, who made up half the town's residents in the colonial era. Archaeologists are still digging at Williamsburg and each year find more fascinating artifacts that tell them about life in the American colonies.

Jamestown, site of the first colonial settlement, has suffered even more than Williamsburg from the passage of time. Today access to the archaeological site is restricted. Still, tourists flock there just to be able to say they visited the first permanent European settlement in the Western

Tourists can find out firsthand what it was like being locked in the stocks in Colonial Williamsburg. It was not much fun for colonists, however, who sometimes had to stand there for hours in all kinds of weather, while passersby sometimes pelted them with rotten vegetables and eggs.

Hemisphere. There is more to do at the re-created Powhatan Indian Village, where tourists participate in many activities showing what life was like in small Indian villages.

Visitors are also drawn to the many beaches of the Tidewater. Virginia Beach was built about 1900 to attract tourists, and in the summer its 29 miles of beaches are dotted with sunbathers. The warm water is perfect for swimming, surfing, and snorkeling.

Norfolk's bustling shipyards are fascinating to anyone interested in warships or the ocean. Nauticus, the National Maritime Center, which opened in 1994, has theaters and hundreds of hands-on exhibits and displays.

The Great Dismal Swamp, south of Norfolk, is a welcome break from the bustle of the city. Most of the swamp is a wildlife refuge where, according to one observer, it is so calm that the "water-snakes glide, the great trees add another ring, the insects rise at sundown, and the most exciting event of the day is photosynthesis." The swamp is home to a very unusual tree, the cypress. It has adapted to its conditions by growing long, skinny roots that come out of the water, with the main part of the tree perched on top of them. These roots help the cypress stay upright in the mud.

The northern part of the Tidewater holds attractions for the many tourists who come to see Washington, D.C. Each year thousands visit Arlington National Cemetery, the nation's largest military cemetery and the site of the graves of President John F. Kennedy and his brother Robert Kennedy as well as the Tomb of the Unknown Soldier. The Pentagon, which houses the U.S. Department of Defense, is also located in Arlington.

A sign on the outskirts of Winchester, a suburb of Washington, says, "Welcome to the Apple Capital of the World." There are many orchards in the area, so it is no surprise that each spring Winchester hosts one of the oldest celebrations in Virginia, the Shenandoah Apple

More than 285,000 veterans from America's various wars are buried at Arlington National Cemetery.

Blossom Festival. Highlights of the festival are a fifty-float parade and the crowning of the apple blossom queen. There is also the Fire Fighters' Parade, the largest display of fire-fighting equipment in the country. Sally Goldfarb, a native of Winchester, calls the festival a "huge deal—as soon as it's over the town starts planning for the next one. My cousin was Miss Apple Blossom, which is a qualifying title for the Miss Virginia pageant. I was Miss Gainesboro Fire Company!"

AN AMERICAN ORIGINAL:
THE CHESAPEAKE BAY RETRIEVER

Only one breed of sporting dog comes from America: the Chesapeake Bay retriever. No one is sure of the "Chessie's" exact ancestry. Mainly a retriever, it is also a mixture of several other breeds.

A favorite story of the retriever's origin is that two dogs, rescued from a wrecked English ship in 1807, were bred to produce the first of this breed. It is more likely that hunters living along the Chesapeake Bay carefully bred this dog to suit their purposes. And the dog is perfect for anyone hunting the many ducks of the Chesapeake Bay. It is large and devoted to retrieving; it doesn't seem to mind being in icy cold water; and its brown color blends into the surroundings, making it difficult for ducks to spot.

The Chessie is related to the Labrador, although it has longer legs and is more slender than its cousin. The biggest difference, however, is in the coat. The Chesapeake Bay retriever has a double coat that is wooly, coarse, and practically waterproof. A Chessie can spend a long time in water just above the freezing point, then come out, give itself one good shake, and be dry.

Very few people along the Chesapeake rely on hunting for their food anymore, yet the breed is still very popular. Chessies are intelligent and loyal to their owners. Their intelligence, though, means that they often get bored and can get into mischief if left alone for long periods of time.

PLACES TO SEE

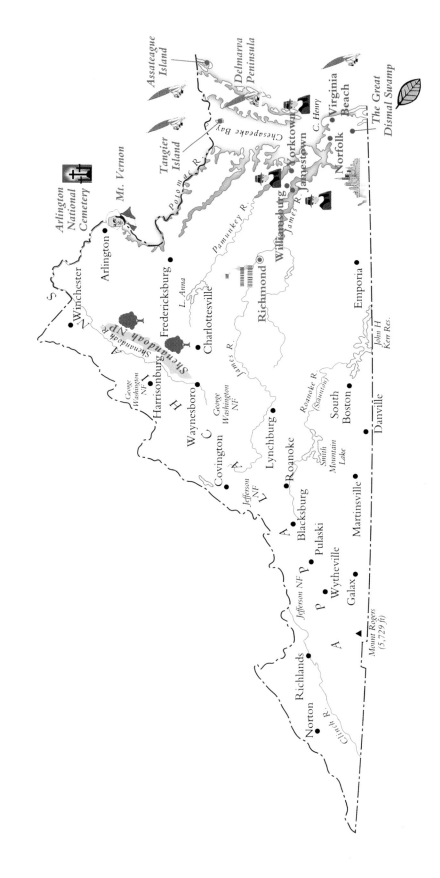

THE PIEDMONT

Virginia's capital city, Richmond, is in the eastern part of the Piedmont. The city was founded in 1682 and became the state's capital in 1780. It was also the capital of the Confederacy during the Civil War. It is now the fourth-largest city in the state (after Virginia Beach, Norfolk, and Chesapeake).

For Kapanga Kasongo, the most fascinating section of Richmond is the Fan, where many historic buildings and art museums are found. He was impressed when an exhibit of African art came to the city, and he took his three small daughters to see it. Thousands of miles from his native Congo, his children could see art made by people from his homeland. He calls Richmond "a very enriching kind of city in terms of all it has to offer, for example, the arts. And in terms of activities, there are all sorts of things going on."

Richmond's science museum includes an optical-illusion room, which makes people look bigger, or smaller, than they actually are.

TEN LARGEST CITIES

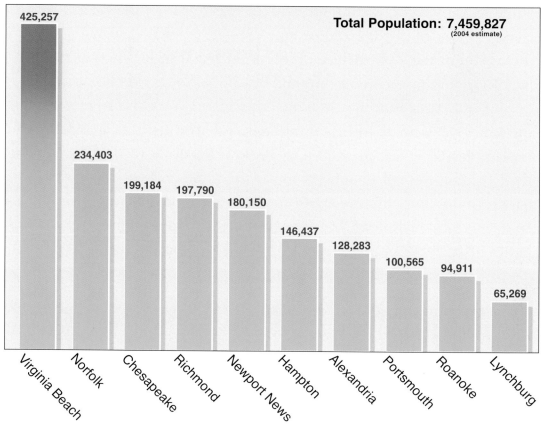

Total Population: 7,459,827
(2004 estimate)

- Virginia Beach — 425,257
- Norfolk — 234,403
- Chesapeake — 199,184
- Richmond — 197,790
- Newport News — 180,150
- Hampton — 146,437
- Alexandria — 128,283
- Portsmouth — 100,565
- Roanoke — 94,911
- Lynchburg — 65,269

Certainly the historic buildings of Richmond are one of the hallmarks of the city. The state capitol was designed by Thomas Jefferson and now houses statues of all eight Virginia-born presidents. Museums include the Museum of the Confederacy, Richmond's City Life Museum, and the Science Museum of Virginia, one of the largest science museums in the country. Here visitors can try their hand at hundreds of interactive exhibits.

THE BIRTH OF A PARK

The area that makes up Shenandoah National Park has been inhabited by people since the Stone Age. Early Indians gathered food there, although they probably formed no permanent settlements.

Next, Europeans settled in the Shenandoah. The beautiful, straight hardwood trees provided ideal building materials, and soon most of the original growth had been cut down. The land was poor for farming, and by the nineteenth century homesteaders had used up all the fertile land on the mountain slopes. The thin mountain soil was washed away by the farming and the increased population. Then, later in the nineteenth century, many of the chestnut trees, which made up about 25 percent of the hardwoods in the region, were killed by a fungus.

Concerned with the destruction of this beautiful area, Congress declared that money be raised to fund a park. Virginia contributed more than $2 million to buy the property of the two thousand people living there. Although some resisted, eventually all of them moved away. The park was dedicated in 1936. Today Shenandoah National Park is starting to return to the condition it was in when Europeans first set foot there.

Also of interest is the historic business area of First and Marshall streets, the site of America's first black-owned bank and insurance company. The area is known as the Wall Street of Black America.

The city of Charlottesville, located in the Piedmont, owes its importance to its most famous citizen, Thomas Jefferson. He founded the University of Virginia in Charlottesville in 1819 and designed the buildings of the main campus. These gracious structures are similar to Jefferson's home, Monticello, which he also designed. Construction on the thirty-five-room house began in 1770 and took forty years to complete. Jefferson hated stairs, so he put all the important rooms on the first floor. The few staircases are only 24 inches wide!

Jefferson was an inventor as well as a statesman and architect and created many innovations in his home to suit his own tastes. For example, in the 1700s clocks had to be wound every day. Jefferson invented a clock that needed winding only once a week. He made a copying devise, with two pens joined together by a bar. When paper is put under both pens, a person can write with just one of them and create a copy at the same time with the other pen. Jefferson also experimented with agriculture. His gardens are still planted with the same kinds of flowers and vegetables he first introduced there.

THE MOUNTAIN AND VALLEY REGION

The Blue Ridge Mountains are the main attraction in this part of the state. Ethel-Marie Underhill, who has lived in eight states and three foreign countries, calls this area "undoubtedly the most beautiful place we have ever lived in." Susan McArthur agrees, saying that what she loves most about her adopted state is "how beautiful it is physically."

All native American horses died out around 15,000 years ago. Modern-day horses, like this one in Flint Hill, are descendants of animals brought over from Europe starting in the 1400s.

Backpackers pause to take in just one of the many spectacular sights Virginia has to offer.

One of the most spectacular attractions is the 200,000-acre Shenandoah National Park, whose name comes from an Indian word meaning "daughter of the stars." About 2 million people visit the park each year. Many visitors participate in the guided walks and tours offered by the park service to educate people about the ecosystem of the area.

Other natural wonders include the Cumberland Gap National Historical Park in the southwestern corner of the state near its border with Kentucky and Tennessee. This gap, or low spot in the Appalachians, allowed settlers moving west to get their heavy wagons to the other side of the mountains.

Adventurous tourists enjoy exploring the area's many limestone caverns. Limestone dissolves in water, so the many underground springs have carved out huge caves. There are also many waterfalls and mineral springs.

Roanoke is home to the Transportation Museum, which traces the history of the railroads. Old steam engines and cabooses are set up outside to be boarded and explored. The museum also has a collection of historic cars—in fact, of anything dealing with transportation.

From history to music, scenery to seafood, foxhunts to ethnic festivals, and politics to art, Virginia has it all. The state's unofficial motto is Virginia Is for Lovers. Not only Virginians, but the many people who visit the state are bound to fall in love with it.

THE FLAG: The state flag, which shows the state seal on a blue background, was first adopted in 1931.

THE SEAL: Although officially adopted in 1931, the state seal was designed in 1776. It shows the Roman goddess Virtus, representing the state, standing over the fallen body of Tyranny. The goddess holds a spear and a sword. The fallen Tyranny holds a whip and a chain, and his crown lies on the ground nearby. The state name appears at the top of the seal; the state motto, Thus Always to Tyrants, appears along the bottom. A circle of Virginia creeper borders the figures.

State Survey

Statehood: June 25, 1788

Origin of Name: Named by Sir Walter Raleigh in honor of Queen Elizabeth I, the Virgin Queen.

Nickname: Old Dominion, Mother of States, Mother of Presidents

Capital: Richmond

Motto: *Sic Semper Tyrannis* ("Thus Always to Tyrants")

Bird: Cardinal

Dog: American foxhound

Flower and Tree: Flowering dogwood

Shell: Oyster

Boat: Chesapeake Bay deadrise

Dance: Square dance

Insect: Tiger swallowtail butterfly

Fish: Brook trout

Fossil: *Chesapecten jeffersonius*

Beverage: Milk

Cardinal

CARRY ME BACK TO OLD VIRGINIA

James A. Bland wrote "Carry Me Back to Old Virginny" in 1875. It became the official state song in 1940. Bland, who toured Europe and the United States with minstrel groups in the 1880s, wrote some seven hundred songs, including such all-time favorites as "Oh, Dem Golden Slippers," "In the Evening by the Moonlight," and "Hand Me My Walking Cane."

When Bland wrote the lyrics to "Carry Me Back to Old Virginny," he used some words that we object to today. In 1997 the state senate voted to retire the song. In the following version you will find suggested changes.

Words and Music by James A. Bland

GEOGRAPHY

Highest Point: 5,729 feet above sea level, at Mount Rogers

Lowest Point: Sea level along the Atlantic coast

Area: 42,769 square miles

Greatest Distance, North to South: 200 miles

Greatest Distance, East to West: 470 miles

Bordering States: West Virginia and Maryland to the north, Kentucky to the west, and North Carolina and Tennessee to the south

Hottest Recorded Temperature: 110° F at Balcony Falls on July 15, 1954

Coldest Recorded Temperature: -30° F at Mountain Lake Bio Station on January 22, 1985

Average Annual Precipitation: 43 inches

Major Rivers: Potomac, Rappahannock, Rapidan, Anna, Pamunkey, James, Roanoke, Dan, Meherrin, Nottoway, Clinch, Holston, Powell, New, Shenandoah

Red fox

Major Lakes: Smith Mountain, John Kerr, Anna, Claytor, Chesdin, Drummond, Moomaw, John W. Flannagan, Lake of the Woods, Monticello, Philpott, Leesville, South Holston

Trees: pine, birch, ash, oak, locust, poplar, sweet gum, black tupelo

Wild Plants: mountain laurel, rhododendron, azalea, Virginia bluebell, black-eyed Susan, Queen Anne's lace, butterfly weed

Animals: white-tailed deer, black bear, red fox, opossum, skunk, raccoon, rabbit, weasel, mink, bobcat, squirrel, beaver, river otter, wild pony

Birds: cardinal, pileated woodpecker, blue jay, robin, woodcock, tern, ibis, wild turkey, quail, mourning dove, swift, ruffed grouse, bald eagle, peregrine falcon, hummingbird, oriole, duck, snow goose

Fish: American eel, bass, bluegill, bowfin, sunfish, perch, catfish, crappie, carp, trout, sea bass, striped bass, sea trout, bluefish, flounder, croaker, hogfish, menhaden

Wild turkey

Endangered Animals: Appalachian monkeyface pearlymussel, birdwing pearlymussel, cracking pearlymussel, Cumberland monkeyface pearly-mussel, Cumberlandian combshell, Delmarva Peninsula fox squirrel, dromedary pearlymussel, duskytail darter, dwarf wedgemussel, fanshell, finback whale, finerayed pigtoe, gray bat, green blossom pearlymussel, hawksbill sea turtle, humpback whale, Indiana bat, James spinymussel, Kemp's ridley sea turtle, leatherback sea turtle, Lee County cave isopod, littlewing pearlymussel, oyster mussel, pink mucket pearlymussel, puma, purple bean, red-cockaded woodpecker, right whale, Roanoke logperch, roseate tern, rough pigtoe, rough rabbitsfoot, Shenandoah salamander, shiny pigtoe, shortnose sturgeon, tan riffleshell, Virginia big-eared bat, Virginia fringed mountain snail, Virginia northern flying squirrel

Endangered Plants: harperella, Michaux's sumac, northeastern bulrush, Peter's mountain mallow, shale barren rock-cress, small-anthered bit-tercress, smooth coneflower

TIMELINE

Virginia History

about 1500 Approximately 18,000 Algonquian, Iroquoian, and Siouan Indians live in Virginia

1524 Florentine explorer Giovanni da Verrazano sails along the coast of Virginia

1570 Spanish missionaries found a settlement on the York River

1607 Jamestown founded

1614 John Rolfe exports tobacco from Jamestown

1619 The House of Burgesses meets for the first time

1619 First Africans arrive at Jamestown as indentured servants

1622 Native Americans of the Powhatan Confederacy attack English settlers along the James River, killing 350

1653 Virginia creates Indian reservations in Gloucester, Lancaster, and York counties

1667 A hurricane strikes Jamestown, destroying between 10,000 and 15,000 houses

1676 Bacon's Rebellion

1699 Williamsburg replaces Jamestown as the seat of Virginia government

1716 English settlers enter the Shenandoah Valley

1732 George Washington is born in Westmoreland County

1736 Virginia's first newspaper, the *Virginia Gazette,* starts publication

1755 George Washington appointed commander-in-chief of Virginia forces during the French and Indian War

1775 Patrick Henry delivers his "Give me liberty, or give me death!" speech at Richmond

1775 Virginia's patriots seize Norfolk from the British

1780 Virginia's capital moves from Williamsburg to Richmond

1781 Lord Cornwallis surrenders his British army at Yorktown

1788 Virginia ratifies the U.S. Constitution and becomes the tenth state

1819 Thomas Jefferson founds the University of Virginia at Charlottesville

1831 A slave rebellion led by Nat Turner results in the deaths of about sixty whites before it is crushed with the death of hundreds of blacks

1859 John Brown seizes Harpers Ferry in an attempt to start a slave revolt

1861 Virginia secedes from the Union

1861 The first major battle of the Civil War is fought at Manassas

1865 General Robert E. Lee surrenders his Confederate Army at Appomattox Court House

1870 Virginia reenters the Union

1888 The world's first successful streetcar system begins operating in Richmond

1959 Integration of schools begins in Virginia

1969 Hurricane Camille causes damaging floods in central and western Virginia

1989 L. Douglas Wilder is elected governor of Virginia, becoming the country's first African-American governor

2003 Ships and personnel from the U.S. Navy Atlantic Fleet headquartered in Norfolk return to bases in Virginia after Operation Iraqi Freedom

ECONOMY

Natural Resources: timber, limestone, dolomite, sand and gravel, quartzite, coal, oil, natural gas

Agricultural Products: hay, soybeans, corn, wheat, apples, peaches, grapes, strawberries, potatoes, tomatoes, peanuts, cotton, tobacco, broiler chickens, beef cattle, hogs

Manufacturing: transportation equipment, textiles, food products, electronic and telecommunications equipment, printed products, chemicals, drugs, robotics, navigation equipment

Business and Trade: wholesale trade, retail trade, transportation, government, banking

Farmworker with unripe tomatoes

CALENDAR OF CELEBRATIONS

George Washington's Birthday (Alexandria) This celebration, held the February weekend of Washington's birthday, includes a Revolutionary War encampment and a parade with two hundred floats, marching bands, and fife-and-drum corps. http://oha.ci.alexandria.va.us/oha-main/alex250/oha-250-highlights.html

Highland Maple Festival (Monterey) Held the second and third weekends in March, this festival features demonstrations on the making of maple syrup. There are also lots of maple-flavored treats to eat. http://lcweb.loc.gov/bicentennial/propage/VA/va-6_h_goodlatte2.html

Virginia Arts Festival (Norfolk) This monthlong celebration of the arts, with music, dance, theater, and more, includes a festival in Colonial Williamsburg. http://www.virginiaartsfest.com/index.html

Dogwood Festival (Charlottesville) This two-week-long April festival celebrates the blooming of the dogwood trees with music, a quilt show, and athletic events. http://www.dogwoodfestival.org/

Shenandoah Apple Blossom Festival (Winchester) In early May apple orchards in the Shenandoah Valley are in full bloom. This weekend festival includes music, parades, rides, and a carnival. http://www.sabf.org/

George Washington's Birthday

Jamestown Landing Day

Jamestown Landing Day (Jamestown) Held in May, this celebration features sailing demonstrations and costumed actors playing the roles of Jamestown settlers. http://www.historyisfun.org/news/calendar.cfm

Harborfest (Norfolk) This weekend festival in June celebrates Norfolk's place by the sea. Tall ships sail into the harbor, and there are sailboat races and fireworks. http://www.norfolkdowntown.com/events/

James River Batteau Festival (Lynchburg) This eight-day-long festival in June features a boat race down the James River in old-fashioned traders' boats, or *bateaux*. Visitors can also enjoy music, crafts, and games. http://www.batteau.org/

Chincoteague Wild Pony Swim (Chincoteague) Every year in July the wild ponies of Assateague Island are rounded up and swum across the channel to Chincoteague. Events in the festival include the auction of the ponies and a carnival. http://www.assateagueisland.com/ponyswim/ponyswim.htm

Hampton Jazz Festival (Hampton) Great jazz sounds fill Hampton as some of the country's best jazz musicians play at this June festival. http://www.hamptoncoliseum.org/jazz

Virginia Highlands Festival (Abingdon) Appalachian culture is celebrated during this festival held in late July through early August. Appalachian music, art, crafts, and writings are featured. Hot-air balloons also make an appearance. http://www.vahighlandsfestival.org/

Old Fiddlers' Convention (Galax) This August celebration features bluegrass, country, and "mountain" music as well as old-time forms of dancing. http://www.oldfiddlersconvention.com/

Prelude to Victory (Williamsburg) On Labor Day weekend in August or September, George Washington and the Continental Army stop in Williamsburg to re-enact the preparations for the Battle of Yorktown of 1781. While Washington and Rochambeau, the French commander, plan the march to Yorktown, the troops practice their shooting and horse-riding skills.

Virginia State Fair (Richmond) The State Fair, held every September, features entertainment, rides, exhibits on Virginia's farm products, and a pioneer homestead. http://www.statefair.com/

Oyster Festival (Urbanna) Visitors can try oysters prepared in a variety of different ways at this November festival. There are also tall ships, parades, and oyster boats to explore. http://www.urbannaoysterfestival.com/

Grand Illumination (Williamsburg) The holiday season in December begins when candles are lit throughout the town and fireworks are launched. Caroling and dancing are part of the celebration too.

STATE STARS

William Howard Armstrong (1914–1999), born in Lexington, was a writer of children's books. His most famous novel is *Sounder.*

Arthur Ashe (1943–1993) was, in 1975, the first African-American man to win the singles title at the Wimbledon tennis tournament. Born in Richmond, Ashe spent the last years of his life working to raise funds to find a cure for AIDS, with which he was accidentally infected during a blood transfusion.

Arthur Ashe

Pearl Bailey (1918–1990), born in Newport News, was an accomplished singer and actress. She is most famous for her roles in the Broadway musical *Hello Dolly* and the movie version of *Porgy and Bess.*

Warren Beatty (1937–   ), a film actor and director, was born in Richmond. He received an Academy Award for directing the film *Reds.* His acting credits include *Dick Tracy* and *Bugsy.*

Richard E. Byrd

Richard E. Byrd (1888–1957) gained fame as an Arctic and Antarctic explorer. Born in Winchester, he was, in 1926, one of the first people to fly over the North Pole.

Willa Cather (1873–1947) won the Pulitzer Prize for her novel *One of Ours.* Born in Winchester, Cather's other books include *O Pioneers!* and *My Antonia.*

George Rogers Clark (1752–1818) was born near Charlottesville. A commander of Virginia troops during the Revolutionary War, Clark led daring raids into the Illinois country and captured the British forts at Kaskaskia, Vincennes, and Cahokia.

William Clark (1770–1838) was the younger brother of George Rogers Clark. William Clark, along with Meriwether Lewis, commanded the expedition sent by Thomas Jefferson to explore the Louisiana Territory in 1804.

Patsy Cline (1932–1963) was a popular country singer whose career was cut short by her death in a plane crash. Born in Winchester, Cline's hits included "Crazy" and "Sweet Dreams."

Patsy Cline

Katie Couric (1957–) is a popular broadcast journalist. She was born in Arlington and has been cohost of NBC's *Today Show* since 1991.

Rita Dove (1952–) was born in Ohio. Since 1989 she has taught at the University of Virginia. Her collection of poems entitled *Thomas and Beulah* won the Pulitzer Prize for poetry in 1987. She is the youngest person and the only African American to serve as poet laureate of the United States.

Ella Fitzgerald (1918–1996), the "First Lady of Song," was born in Newport News. Fitzgerald won eight Grammy Awards for her jazz singing.

Patrick Henry (1736–1799) of "Give me liberty, or give me death" fame was born in Hanover County. Henry served two terms as governor of Virginia and led the fight to have the Bill of Rights added to the U.S. Constitution.

Thomas "Stonewall" Jackson

Thomas "Stonewall" Jackson (1824–1863), one of the most famous Confederate generals, was born in Clarksburg. Jackson earned his nickname at the First Battle of Bull Run when another Confederate rallied his own troops by exclaiming, "There is Jackson standing like a stone wall."

Thomas Jefferson (1743–1826), the author of the Declaration of Independence and third president of the United States, was born in Albermarle County. Jefferson was also an architect and an inventor. He designed his home at Monticello, many of the buildings at the University of Virginia, and the Virginia state capitol in Richmond. Jefferson's inventions included the swivel chair and a clock that told the day of the week as well as the time.

Robert E. Lee (1807–1870), born in Stratford, was the commander of the Confederate Army during the Civil War. A brilliant military leader, Lee became the president of Washington College, today known as Washington and Lee University, after the war.

Meriwether Lewis (1774–1809), along with William Clark, was named by President Thomas Jefferson to explore the Louisiana Territory in 1804. Lewis was born in Albermarle County and served as governor of the Louisiana Territory after exploring there.

Shirley MacLaine (1934–   ) was born in Richmond. An actress, dancer, and author, MacLaine's many films include *Terms of Endearment,* for which she received a Best Actress Oscar in 1983, and *Steel Magnolias.*

James Madison (1751–1836), the fourth president of the United States, was born in Port Conway. Madison is known as the Father of the Constitution for his part in writing that document. He also helped write the Bill of Rights to the U.S. Constitution.

Moses Malone (1955–   ) was born and grew up in Petersburg. Malone was the first person to become a professional basketball player straight out of high school. A great jumper, Malone led the NBA in rebounding six times and was later inducted into the Hall of Fame.

Cyrus Hall McCormick (1809–1884), born in Rockbridge County, revolutionized farming with his invention of a mechanical reaper.

McCormick's machine allowed one farmer to do the work of five when harvesting wheat.

William Holmes McGuffey (1800–1873), a famous educator, was a professor at the University of Virginia. McGuffey wrote a series of books, known as McGuffey Readers, that were used to teach reading in American schools for many years.

Cyrus Hall McCormick

James Monroe (1758–1831), the fifth president of the United States, was born in Westmoreland County. Monroe had also served as a U.S. senator, governor of Virginia, and U.S. secretary of state.

Pocahontas (1595?–1617), meaning either "playful one" or "favorite daughter," was the nickname of the Powhatan princess Matoaka. According to legend, Pocahontas saved the life of settler John Smith of Jamestown as he was about to be executed by the Powhatan. Pocahontas later married settler John Rolfe and became known as Lady Rebecca Rolfe.

Edgar Allan Poe (1809–1849) spent his childhood in Richmond and returned there later as a writer for a magazine. Poe is famous for his detective and horror stories, as well as his poetry. His works include "The Raven" and "The Pit and the Pendulum."

Bill "Bojangles" Robinson

Bill "Bojangles" Robinson (1878–1949) was a well-known dancer and actor. Robinson danced in a number of Broadway musicals, as well as in several films. He was born in Richmond.

Kate Smith (1909–1986), singer and actress, is best known for her singing of "God Bless America." During the 1940s, Smith was called the First Lady of American Radio. She was born in Greenville.

Jeb Stuart (1833–1864), born in Patrick County, was named James Ewell Brown Stuart but was always known by his initials. He commanded the cavalry brigade of the Army of Northern Virginia during the Civil War. General Lee called this brilliant general the "eyes of the army."

Maggie Walker (1867–1934) was born the daughter of a slave in Richmond. Walker became the first woman bank president in the United States after opening a bank in Richmond.

Booker T. Washington (1856–1915) was born a slave on a tobacco plantation in Franklin County. Washington later founded Tuskegee Institute in Alabama, a college for African Americans, and was a leading spokesperson for blacks. His autobiography, *Up from Slavery,* has become a classic.

George Washington (1732–1799), the first president of the United States, was born in Westmoreland County. Washington led the colonial army during the Revolutionary War and served as president of the Constitutional Convention before being elected the country's first president.

Woodrow Wilson

L. Douglas Wilder (1931–   ), elected governor of Virginia in 1989, was born in Richmond. He was the first African American to be elected governor in the United States.

Woodrow Wilson (1856–1924), the twenty-eighth president of the United States, was born in Staunton. Wilson also served as president of Princeton University and governor of New Jersey. He received the Nobel Peace Prize in 1919 for his work in helping to establish the League of Nations.

Tom Wolfe (1930–   ) is a multi-award-winning author who was born in Richmond. He is known for both nonfiction *(The Right Stuff)* and fiction *(The Bonfire of the Vanities)*.

FUN FACTS

Norfolk's recycling program created "Mount Trashmore," a mountain of trash that was turned into a children's playground.

The Pentagon in Arlington, the main offices of the U.S. Department of Defense, has almost 18 miles of corridors.

Richard Henry Lee and Francis Lightfoot Lee of Westmoreland County were the only brothers to sign the Declaration of Independence.

The country's oldest sporting event is the Natural Chimneys Jousting Tournament, held every August at Natural Chimneys Regional Park. Contestants use lances to catch steel rings while riding on horseback.

The Memorial Day holiday originated when a group of schoolgirls began placing flowers on the graves of Civil War soldiers in Petersburg.

Virginia has more miles of trout streams than it has roads.

William Henry Harrison of Virginia served the shortest term of any U.S. president. Harrison caught a cold on the day he was inaugurated and died of pneumonia a month later. John Tyler, another Virginian, then took over the presidency.

Bill "Bojangles" Robinson of Richmond was a famous dancer of the early twentieth century. He could also run backward very fast and set a record by running backward 75 yards in 8.2 seconds.

Arlington National Cemetery

In a custom that dates back to the 1600s, Mattaponi and Pamunkey Indians still present Virginia's governor with a number of gifts every year instead of paying taxes. The gifts include three arrows; wild game such as deer, turkey, and fish; and pottery and baskets.

In 1861 Wilmer McLean moved his family from the Manassas area to get away from the Civil War after his house was damaged in the First Battle of Bull Run. The McLeans moved to the quiet town of Appomattox Court House in south-central Virginia. Four years later Robert E. Lee surrendered to Ulysses S. Grant in the McLeans' living room.

Robert E. Lee's favorite horse, Traveller, is buried next to Lee's grave at Washington and Lee University in Lexington.

Endless Caverns near New Market include formations named Snowdrift, Fairyland, and Grand Canyon. No one has ever discovered the starting point in this maze of caverns.

The Blue Ridge Mountains are so named because, from a distance, the trees that cover them appear to be blue.

TOUR THE STATE

Arlington National Cemetery (Arlington) This cemetery for the nation's military dead is an impressive sight, with row upon row of simple white headstones. The cemetery also contains the grave of John F. Kennedy, the Tomb of the Unknown Soldier, and Arlington House, Robert E. Lee's home before the Civil War.

Manassas National Battlefield (Manassas) The site of the first major battle of the Civil War has been preserved and looks much as it did in 1861.

Mount Vernon (Mount Vernon) George Washington acquired this plantation house on the Potomac River in 1754. Today the mansion has been restored to look as it did in the last year of Washington's life.

Chincoteague National Wildlife Refuge (Assateague Island) Visitors can view the many birds that inhabit the refuge from the Wildlife Loop, a 3.25-mile trail for pedestrians, cars, and bicycles. Special bus tours go into areas of the refuge not open to cars.

Stratford Hall Plantation (Stratford) Built in the 1730s, Stratford Hall was the birthplace of Robert E. Lee. The plantation grounds include woods, gardens, and cultivated fields, all restored to look as they did in the early 1800s.

The Museum of the Confederacy (Richmond) Collections at this museum include equipment and clothing that belonged to Robert E. Lee, "Stonewall" Jackson, and other Confederate leaders.

Colonial Williamsburg Historical Area (Williamsburg) This re-creation of the eighteenth-century town includes the governor's palace, the capitol, the courthouse, and numerous houses and taverns.

Jamestown Settlement (Jamestown) Costumed guides explain life in this reproduction of Virginia's earliest settlement. The ships that brought the first settlers and a Powhatan Indian village are also re-created.

Yorktown Victory Center (Yorktown) This museum of the American Revolution includes a Continental Army camp and a timeline walkway called "Road to Revolution."

The Mariners' Museum (Newport News) Visitors can explore the history of humans on the sea, including special exhibits of artifacts from the Civil War ironclad ship the *Monitor* and carved figureheads from sailing ships.

Nauticus, the National Maritime Center (Norfolk) Shipbuilding, environmental science, and the U.S. Navy are only a few of the maritime subjects that can be explored at Nauticus. Visitors can take command of a navy ship in a battle simulation.

Virginia Museum of Natural History (Martinsville) Visitors can see a computer-animated triceratops as well as other exhibits showcasing Virginia's natural history.

Pocahontas Exhibition Coal Mine (Pocahontas) This exhibition coal mine explains the history of coal mining in the region and includes demonstrations of coal cutting and blasting.

Cumberland Gap National Historical Park (Ewing) The road that cuts through the park closely follows the one blazed by Daniel Boone. Hiking trails and paved roads lead to scenic overlooks.

Natural Bridge (Natural Bridge) One of the Seven Natural Wonders of the World, the Natural Bridge is a limestone arch 90 feet long and 215 feet high.

Naval Station Norfolk (Norfolk) Visitors can take a guided bus tour of the naval installations, home port to more than seventy-five navy ships and several aircraft squadrons.

Children's Museum of Virginia (Portsmouth) Lots of hands-on exhibits at this museum provide fun learning experiences for both kids and adults.

Virginia Marine Science Museum (Virginia Beach) Visitors can explore a Chesapeake Bay habitat through an aquarium exhibit that includes black drum, striped bass, and flounder. Other exhibits allow visitors to create a fish on a computer and take a walk over a salt marsh.

Appomattox Court House National Historical Park (Appomattox) This village of twenty-seven buildings has been restored to look as it did in 1865 when Confederate general Robert E. Lee surrendered his army to Union general Ulysses S. Grant.

Monticello (Charlottesville) Thomas Jefferson designed Monticello and lived there from 1770 until his death in 1826. The grounds include vineyards, an orchard, and a garden like that kept by Jefferson.

Booker T. Washington National Monument (Roanoke) This site re-creates the daily life Washington would have known in his early years as a slave on a small tobacco plantation in Virginia.

Frontier Culture Museum

Frontier Culture Museum (Staunton) Seventeenth- and eighteenth-
century working farms from England, northern Ireland, and Germany
are re-created here. A nineteenth-century American farm shows how
the cultures have blended. Costumed interpreters add to the fun at this
living-history museum.

Luray Caverns (Luray) Caverns here range from 30 to 140 feet high and
include gigantic rock formations. The Stalacpipe Organ uses stalactites
to create music.

Shenandoah National Park (Front Royal) Hundreds of miles of hiking paths
and the breathtaking Skyline Drive highlight this beautiful national park.

Find Out More

If you would like to learn more about Virginia, look for the following titles in your library, bookstore, or video store.

BOOKS

Blashfield, Jean. *Virginia.* Chicago: Children's Press, 1999.

Cocke, William. *A Historical Album of Virginia.* Brookfield, CT: Millbrook Press, 1995.

De Angelis, Gina. *Virginia.* Chicago: Children's Press, 2001.

Fritz, Jean. *The Double Life of Pocahontas.* New York: Putnam, 1983. (A factual account of the life of Pocahontas both before and after the settlers' arrival.)

Heinrichs, Ann. *Virginia.* Mankato, MN: Compass Point Books, 2002.

Henry, Marguerite. *Misty of Chincoteague.* Chicago: Rand McNally, 1947. (The award-winning story of two children who buy a foal at the Chincoteague pony roundup.)

O'Connell, Kim A. *Virginia.* Berkeley Heights, NJ: Enslow, 2003.

Pollack, Pamela, and Jean Craven. *Virginia: The Old Dominion.* Milwaukee: Gareth Stevens, 2001.

Sakurai, Gail. *The Jamestown Colony.* Chicago: Children's Press, 1997.

Sirvaitis, Karen. *Virginia.* Minneapolis: Lerner, 2002.

Stapen, Candyce H. *Virginia: Family Adventure Guide.* Old Saybrook, CT: The Globe Pequot Press, 1995. (A guidebook that provides historic background and discusses places and activities likely to appeal to young people.)

Virginia Festival Fun for Kids! Atlanta: Carole Marsh Books, Gallopade, 1994.

Virginia Jeopardy! Answers and Questions about Our State. Atlanta: Carole Marsh Books, Gallopade, 1994.

WEB SITES

http://quickfacts.census.gov/qfd/states/51000.html
Quick facts and figures about the state.

http://www.endangeredspecie.com/states/va.htm
Information on endangered species in Virginia.

www.myvirginia.org
The official Web site of the Commonwealth of Virginia.

Your school librarian can help you find the CD-ROMs, videos, videodiscs, and computer software listed here.

VIDEOS AND VIDEODISCS

The Early Colonists. United Learning, Niles, IL.
This video emphasizes the settlements in the Virginia Colony.

The Geography of the Southeastern States. Society for Visual Education.

The American Frontier: Jamestown. Society for Visual Education.

Rediscover America's State Capitals: Richmond, Virginia. City Productions Home Video.

Looking for America: The Southeast. Clearvue/eav, Chicago, IL.

SOFTWARE

Great American States Race. Heartsoft, Tulsa, OK.
This disk (PC or Mac) can be played at three different levels of difficulty.

ABOUT THE AUTHOR

Tracy Barrett is the author of numerous books and magazine articles for young readers, including the multi-award-winning young-adult novel, *Anna of Byzantium* (Random House). Her most recent publications are a middle-grade novel, *On Etruscan Time* (Henry Holt Books for Young Readers), and a nonfiction history text, *The Ancient Greek World* (Oxford University Press). She teaches courses on writing for children and on children's literature and makes presentations to students, librarians, and teachers. She is on the faculty of Vanderbilt University in Nashville, Tennessee, where she lives with her husband and two teenagers. Find out more at www.tracybarrett.com.

Index

Page numbers in boldface are illustrations and charts.